Inspired by true events

# BlacKout

the novel

Written By Essence Bestselling Author

## Anthony Whyte

Based on screenplay by

## Jerry LaMothe

AUGUSTUS
PUBLISHING

**CASWELL**
COMMUNICATIONS

HU

This is a work of fiction. Names, characters, places, and incidents are products of the author's imagination or are used fictitiously and are not to be construed as real. Any resemblance to actual events, locales or organizations, or persons, living or dead is entirely coincidental.

Produced by Judith Aidoo
Screenplay by Jerry LaMothe
Novel by Anthony Whyte
Edited by Parijat Desai
Design by Jason Claiborne

Augustus Publishing paperback May 2009

 **CASWELL** COMMUNICATIONS

**AugustusPublishing.com**
info@augustuspublishng.com

# BlacKout

# PROLOGUE

Thursday, August 14, 2003, 4pm

No one could imagine that a sequence of electrical mishaps would trigger the worst blackout in the U.S. history. Millions of Americans in the northeast were without power for up to forty eight hours. In New York City, police commissioner, Raymond W. Kelly, reported that the first window broke on Flatbush Avenue in Brooklyn, at about 4:20 p.m. on August 14, 2003, about 10 minutes after the blackout began.

Some New Yorkers were in shock and compared the catastrophic event to 9/11. Many were prepared and worked to help fellow New Yorkers. While others were not in such a giving mood, looters were out, price gouging was rampant and accidental fires were severe.

There were 56 break-ins, the police identified as looting, smash-and-grab type situation. Looters struck groceries, shoe stores and appliance stores, stealing goods and cash. There were 11 shootings during the blackout. Between the time of the blackout 4:15 p.m.

Thursday and 5:00 a.m. Saturday, there were six homicides. There were 96,660 calls to 911 during the blackout almost a third coming in the first three hours, before 7 p.m. on Thursday, August 14, 2003. The police responded to 26,000 radio runs.

The top five precincts reporting burglaries were the 70th which includes the neighborhoods of Flatbush and Crown Heights, the 67th in East Flatbush, the 73rd in Bedford Stuyvesant and Brownsville. The worst of the 48 hours of hell and looting was concentrated in the central parts of Brooklyn.

Overall public officials characterized the blackout as peaceful but it was real different for residents of Browser Street apartments. Framed between Flatbush and Browser Street, these apartment buildings were separated by a small subway station from the notorious Hallsboro Projects. A relatively stable East Flatbush Brooklyn community underwent a hail of dramatic events that would change lives forever.

# ONE

**August 14, 2003, 8:00 a.m.**

The people of Flatbush, Brooklyn awoke to the sweltering heat coming off the top of the apartment buildings. Sunshine and high humidity locked the city in a ferocious heat vice. Craving relief, the residents of Browser Street migrated from their apartments to enjoy the fresh air outdoors.

It was around 9 a.m. when three women of West Indian descent sat on lawn chairs blocking the entrance to 254 Browser Street. They were busy chatting up the latest gossip, while keeping their eyes on the crowd of teens surrounding Tech. He was in front of the barbershop hawking his CDs and DVDs.

"I got it all," Tech shouted. "From the latest Fifty to classic Biggie, some new Jay-Z, I got it … I got it!"

By 10:00 a.m., Corey was on his way to the barbershop to get a haircut, and stepped to Tech with a request.

"What it do? You have the new *Bad Boys II* soundtrack?" Corey asked checking out Tech's display.

"I got it right here, dog!" Tech said handing the CD to Corey. "That joint's bananas," Tech added as Corey examined the disk. "It's selling like crack all day long, everyday," Tech said pushing his sales pitch.

"Hmm...word? What it do?" Corey asked.

"On n' poppin'! Cop it. It's jumpin'. And you need this Sean Paul remix and the G-Unit and Fifty Cent joint... Fire!" Tech said placing two CDs in Corey's hand.

"Ahight, I hear you," Corey said looking at each CD and quickly passing a twenty dollar bill to Tech.

"And I got the new Freddy versus Jason on DVD, director's cut! Fire! What you know about that?"

"Damn! That joint ain't due out for another couple weeks," Corey said scratching his head, visibly impressed.

"What's my muthafucking name, dog?" Tech asked.

"Ahight, you do what ya do, dogs," Corey said smiling and giving Tech a pound.

Nelson and Rick lifted the gate to the barbershop, triggering a sudden flight of pigeons from their overnight perches.

"Whew, its gonna be a mother of a hot one today. You feel the heat already?" Nelson observed, shielding his eyes and gazing at the bright sun.

"Yeah, no doubt. I'm sayin' my brother, may we shine like the sun," Rick nodded in agreement. "Hope we get a lot of heads today," he added walking inside and dusting off his barber chair.

"What it do?" Corey greeted, walking into the barbershop. "I need a fresh one for the weekend, Rick," he continued, taking a seat in Rick's chair and glancing at the mirror.

The barbershop was the place where everyone who was anyone came to hang out. From the latest cuts to freshest style, anything that was popping happened first at Nelson's barbershop.

Nelson was a proud, thirty-something entrepreneur who owned the barbershop. A vocal leader, he had street savvy with genuine social conscience. He was known to stand up for friends and often went out of his way to give a helping hand. At the same time, Nelson had old-school swagger and was known to get down with his knuckle game. He made his reputation fighting for what he believed in.

Rick, one of Nelson's barbers, was also in his thirties and had the rep of being an entertaining brother. Known for his sometimes arrogant ways, Rick enjoyed yapping about his sexual exploits. His different baby mothers would sometimes show up at the barbershop bringing drama. Most of the customers just laughed at his calamities, while he busily laced another satisfied customer with the latest fresh haircut.

Cam was the only female hanging in the group. She was a star athlete in high school, renowned for her basketball prowess. Her talent on the court earned her mad respect from the fellas. She wasn't at the barbershop for haircuts; it was simply her favorite hangout. Not only did Cam enjoy hanging with them, she also dressed like one of the guys, sporting baggy jeans, T-shirt and corn rows.

"Damn, look at the ass on shortie in that video! She doin' what she do," Corey said pointing to the television screen.

For a few rump-shaking seconds, all eyes turned to look at the latest Jigga video playing on BET.

"You know I heard them chicks don't make a dime, shaking ass in those videos, you feeling me?" Nelson announced.

"I don't know about all that. I know they gotta to be eating. I used to date one of'em video-hos, I mean 'chicks', and I'm sayin', the bitch was getting paid," Rick said smiling.

"Yeah, video-ho is right. They getting paid for their services off camera, that's what's really up," Cam said sucking her teeth.

"Sounds a little like hatin', you feel me, Cam?" Nelson smirked.

"Please, I don't love 'em ho's. I likes me a gangsta bitch. I like'em pretty but gangsta, that's what's up," Cam smiled.

"Damn, I'm sayin', you might as well just date a dude," Rick said with a chuckle.

Cam's explanation was drowned by raucous laughter. She resigned herself to throwing up her two middle fingers.

Tech took a break from hustling and walked into the barbershop. He and Nelson were very good friends and shared much history. Both had played on the same high school basketball team and came up hustling drugs with each other. After getting caught up with the law, they both got out the game.

Besides selling mixed CDs, Tech also functioned as the manager for budding rapper L. Tech not only assisted with sales and marketing of his new CD, he was also helping to get L signed to a recording deal with a major label. Tech worked at a friend's makeshift recording studio on Flatbush Avenue and was able to print a couple thousand CDs and sell them. The partnership was going well, but L needed to manage his time better. This is where Tech's help was crucial.

"Where's your boy L? He ain't here yet?" Tech asked Nelson.

"How long have you known L?" Nelson shot back.

"A while now," Tech answered with a chuckle.

"You know that nigga in the bodega messing with them Arabs, or rollin' up sump'n to smoke, " Nelson said.

"That's one hun'red. L's probably at the bodega gettin' a Dutch or sump'n," Tech said.

"You feel me? He does nothing but roll up, gettin' high on bullshit all day long," Nelson laughed.

"He'll be here soon, high as a muthafucka, talking plenty shit. And that's one hun'red," Tech laughed.

The two men exchanged dap like friends who had shared many years of private jokes between them, and Tech went back to work.

"Come get these CDs," Tech shouted to passersby while looking out for L.

# 13 | BlacKout

# TWO

**August 14, 2003, 10:45 a.m.**

The bodega on the corner of Browser Street and Flatbush Avenue was the only grocery store in the neighborhood. A stream of morning customers rapidly moved in and out of its doors. L was on his way to the barbershop where he worked as an apprentice. He picked up some items and walked to the cash register, where Ali, an Americanized Arab in his early twenties, greeted him. Another Middle Eastern man worked the Lotto machine. L put the same items on the counter that he had been buying everyday since the summer started.

"Ali, what up?" L smiled.

"Hey L, how're you doing?" Ali responded smiling.

Ali had been working in the small grocery store since 1997 and was wise to the ways of the residents. He endured much chiding by the likes of L and others. Ali knew it was all in jest and greeted each person with a smile. After coming from Egypt ten years ago, he had made Brooklyn his home. He liked the amenities in the neighborhood and the people who lived there.

" 'Nother day, 'nother hustle…I'm about to go hard body at work. I just can't do it without my newspaper, my ice tea, some chips and…," L said placing each item on the counter. Ali walked away and quickly returned with a Dutchmaster cigar. He handed it to L.

"Whew, this smells fresh. A mornin' puff and I'll be like hard body good, Ali," L smiled.

"Yeah, I hear you. That'll be two-fifty," Ali said watching L pull out two crumpled dollar bills and change. L threw the money on the counter.

"Ahight, let's see what we got here. Ten, fifteen…Ali, I owe you thirty cents," L said.

"No, no! You do this everyday. What is it that you don't understand? No credit! The sign right there says it," Ali said pointing to a poster above the cash register. L stared at the sign as if he had never seen it before. Nodding, he looked impatiently back at Ali.

"Yeah, but I come here hard body, everyday man. That sign only applies to people who don't shop up in here on a reg, right?" L asked.

"No, no, no, it applies to everyone, including you, L," Ali said.

"C'mon Ali, stop fuckin' around, man. You know I'll give you that small change tomorrow," L said reaching for the bag with the items.

"I'm serious L. I can't let you off anymore. Don't you count how much money you have every morning?" Ali ranted.

"C'mon man, we go back way back, hard body like, Ali." L said laughing.

Ali stared at him, wearing a serious frown on his grill. He was trying to make a point and continued without softening his expression.

"Everyday you come in here, go through your pockets, and discover that you don't have enough cash. Maybe if you counted your money before you came in here, you'd realize you don't have enough to buy all you want."

"Don't go so hard for a few cents, my man. You might just bust a vessel. Over what, a few fuckin' cents…?" L joked.

"Okay, how about this? Put the paper back and now I owe you twenty cents. Is that all good?"

"Nah, nah on da real, I'm not feelin' that idea. I can't start the day without readin' the newspaper."

"Ok, put the Dutch back," Ali's frustration was visible.

"You're really buggin' hard body, Ali. C'mon man, stop tryin' a play me. You gettin' rich off us out here. And me personally, you know I be up in here on the daily, now you wanna spaz out on me for thirty fuckin' cents?"

"Hold up, hold up. Who the hell is getting rich? You think I'd be here working sixteen hours a day, if I was rich?"

"Y'all got all that oil. Stop fuckin' spazzin' on thirty cents, man. You really tryin' a embarrass me, for real," L hissed, searching his pockets. "See? I ain't got it."

"And no, I'm not spazzing out for thirty cents. You probably owe me about ten G's by now. That shit accumulates. That's why we don't accept IOU's," Ali said.

"Whateva, man," L said waving him off and grabbing the bag.

"You know what I could do with ten Gs?" Ali asked as L walked out the store.

WELCOME
TO
**BROOKLYN**

**11:00 a.m.**

L stopped to roll his blunt. Scanning the block, he saw the kids at the pizza store. He watched for a few beats then split the Dutchmaster dumping the tobacco out. L crushed the sticky green piff, and evenly poured it down the middle of the blunt. The pizza shop was teeming with teens. They screamed orders while L licked the Dutchmaster, sealed it and thought about getting a slice. Glancing at the fake Rollie on his wrist, L changed his mind.

It was 11:05 a.m. and he was about to spark the blunt but spotted the police posted on both corners. The heavy police presence in the neighborhood made it seem as if the place was under martial law. L hid the blunt as a patrol cruiser slowly rolled by and the undercover cops grilled him with their looks of suspicion.

"You ain't takin' my little weed today," L mumbled under his breath, walking quickly to the barbershop. Nelson would soon be sending Cam or Tech looking for him, L thought as he stashed the blunt. L saw a uniformed officer coming toward him and bounced.

**11:07 a.m.**

It was bubbling hot and fire hydrants were being readied for the rising temperature. Children were chasing each other on bikes and one of them ran into a slightly plump African-American woman dressed in a nurse's uniform. The middle-aged woman was carrying two grocery bags.

"Sorry, Ms. Thompson," one of the mothers sitting and watching, shouted. "Devon, tell Ms. Thompson you're sorry."

"I'm sorry, Ms. Thompson," the boy said, quickly running off to play.

"It's alright, Devon," Ms. Thompson said with a friendly smile but he had already raced out of earshot.

Although exhausted from her graveyard shift at the hospital, Ms. Thompson headed home wearing her wide smile. She had been married but her husband walked out right after her only child, CJ, was born. Ms. Thompson worked in a nursing home while attending college. Her proudest moment came when she completed the RN program at the Brooklyn campus of Long Island University.

Ms. Thompson and CJ, now a teenager, lived in her first floor, two-bedroom apartment at 254 Browser Street. Weary but confident, she was in front of the building they had called home for the past eighteen years.

George, the super was coming out of her building. A tall, strong, and proud man, George was busy taking trash out of the building. He stopped for a minute to catch his breath and wiped sweat from his forehead with a hankerchief. One of the West Indian women seated in front of the building stared at him and he glanced back at them. Their morning ritual was about to begin.

"Super, when you gon' fix mi sink, man? Since last week you come by, but you never come back," she said.

"I haven't forgotten you, Beatrice. I'm still waiting on management to send me the parts. As soon as they come in, you'll be the first on my list," George said politely.

The excuse fell on deaf ears. Beatrice sucked her teeth and gave him a phony smile. She turned to her friends and continued talking.

"That man is full of shit! Let him keep playing with mi. I soon report his butt to the landlord. Didn't you report him a month ago, Sister Carol?" Beatrice asked.

"Cha, you know how many times I reported him already? That man no fool no one. He stays in his apartment and sleep all day long. He don't do not one damn thing, right Ms. Germaine?" Sister Carol said.

"You got that right. All you ever see him do is sweep up out front in the morning, then he throw a little garbage out so people think he's doin' sump'n. That's a nice job, boy. I should fill out an application," Ms. Germaine laughed.

The women snickered in agreement. George heard their comments as he put out the trash.

"Old heffas! Out all day minding other people's business," he whispered under his breath while packing away the day's trash.

"Are you saying something to me, Mr. Super?" Beatrice asked.

"Oh nothing, just an old man talking to himself," George smiled.

It was at 11:10 a.m. and Ms. Thompson arrived in front of the building.

"Good morning, George," she greeted.

"Good morning. How was work?" George said returning her pleasantry.

"Let's just say, I hope my son has some warm water waiting for my feet when I get upstairs, then I'm getting straight in my bed," Ms. Thompson said with a sigh.

"Now that sounds like a plan to me," George said.

They laughed and felt the inquiring stares of the three West Indian women. George and Ms. Thompson turned around and caught the three sticking their noses out, sniffing for information. George's stare caused the inquisitive women to quickly redirect their focus. Ms. Thompson wiped her face with a handkerchief.

"How's CJ doing?" George asked with a friendly smile.

"He's fine, thank you. He should be getting ready for work. He's keeping himself busy until school starts in the fall," Ms. Thompson said.

"Oh, so he decided which school he's going to attend already?" George asked.

"Yes, he'll be going to Penn State in the fall on a full academic scholarship, George," Ms. Thompson beamed.

"God bless him. That's beautiful, you must be proud," George said hugging her.

"Very much so," Ms. Thompson said smiling. "It finally is happening George, my luck is changing. CJ is gonna be fine now."

"I've seen a lot of these kids grow up right in front of my eyes, and it's really a shame how some turned out. I tip my hat to you for what you did," George said, playfully lowering the brim of his cap.

"I'll tell you this much, I just count my blessings because you know, you could do everything right and they still turn on you. It's happened to plenty of my friends," Ms. Thompson said.

"That's true. Well I know you're tired, I don't want to hold you. Go get your rest," George said.

"I will, take care," Ms Thompson said and started toward the building. "Oh by the way, George, I have a leak coming down from my bathroom ceiling…" She winked.

"Hmm, hmm," the West Indian women hemmed when they saw a big grin spreading across George's face.

"I'll be up there in about an hour. How's that…?" George asked glancing at his watch.

"That's fine. Thank you, George," Ms Thompson said and winked again before continuing through the entrance of the building. She stopped and looked at the three ladies sitting out front. "Morning ladies," she said before disappearing into the building.

"Morning, Ms Thompson," the three ladies chorused with very little enthusiasm.

"Did you hear that woman, bragging about her child? Like he the only one doing right. Did I tell you, my Trevor got accepted to college too?" Sister Carol asked.

"Really, but ain't he about thirty?" Beatrice asked.

"So what…? It's never too late," Ms. Germaine said.

"Thank you, Ms. Germaine. Anyway he's taking two night classes at Medgar Evers Community College," Sister Carol continued.

"Good for him. Anyway back to Ms. Show-Off, why she wearing a nurse uniform? Isn't she a housekeeper or something like that?" Beatrice asked.

"No, she's a nurse for real. Her tag says RN. I was going to be one, you know, but I changed my mind. Jesus had another calling for me. Praise the Lord," Ms. Germaine said.

"Well, I hope these people out here don't think I don't work you know, just 'cause I'm sitting out here. I work nights too you know," Sister Carol said.

"You need to be upstairs sleeping, then," Beatrice suggested.

"It's too damn hot," Sister Carol replied.

"I wanna see how quick the super is gonna be up in that woman's apartment," Ms. Germaine blurted.

"You know him gwine to be there as soon as possible," Beatrice said.

"I hear he's been doing more than just fixing leaks in her apartment," Ms. Germaine said.

"Ms. Germaine...!" Beatrice laughed.

"No, no. It's no secret. Everybody knows that was the real reason her husband left her..."

"And I couldn't help but notice the way he was hugging and

feeling her up—" Sister Carol snickered.

"Let me tell you, there's more to it than meets the eye," Ms. Germaine said just as Sister Carol poked her with a knee.

"Shush… you mouth! Him a come, him a come," she said quickly as George came into view. The ladies turned their heads pretending to be interested in something in the other direction.

# THREE

At 11:15 a.m. the alarm clock went off. The jarring sound came from C2, a second floor apartment in Ms. Thompson's building. Inside was Claudine, an attractive Latina woman who lived with her boyfriend James. The ruggedly good-looking, twenty-six year old was in the kitchen busy making breakfast.

It was hot in the apartment. Claudine's face glistened with sweat as she tossed and turned in bed. She was awakened by the music accompanying James' cooking. She peeked at the clock and jumped up from the bed.

"James... James...!" she called out running through the well-kept living room and into the kitchen to find James standing over the stove wearing boxers and a wife-beater.

"Hey, baby," he said turning to her. "Good morning."

"I overslept. I'm going to be so late for work. Why didn't you wake me up?" Claudine said sounding testy.

"Baby, you didn't come to bed till about three in the morning. You were on the computer all night," James said looking at her.

"What does that have to do with anything?" Claudine argued.

"You looked so peaceful this morning I didn't want to bother you. Besides I wanted to surprise you with breakfast in bed," James said.

Her annoyance was clear. He really loved her but there were times when she completely got on his nerves.

"Ah, shit! My boss is gonna kill me!" She screamed storming out.

"C'mon, you can work at home. You do it all the time," James said turning back to the eggs frying on the stove. "How do you want your eggs?" He shouted.

"No thank you."

Disappointed, he shook his head. There was a lot of food and the one person he wished could enjoy it, wouldn't.

"You done killed my whole Mack mood, man," James sighed.

11:22 a.m.

Ms. Thompson fresh home from her work at the Kings County Hospital, settled down in front of the television, remote in hand. Her son CJ came out of the shower and smiled when he saw her.

"Hey Mom," the nineteen-year-old honor student greeted his

mother.

"Hey baby, how was your evening?" Ms. Thompson asked returning his smile.

"Good. And how was work, Mom?"

"Work was work, baby. What time are you going in today?"

"About two-thirty. Friday I'll be going in earlier," CJ answered checking his watch.

"Oh, I'll be asleep," his mother said sounding fatigued. Then she smiled. "You sound like you're going to be making some money to take your Mommy out on the weekend."

"I know your birthday is coming up soon and you have to work," CJ winked.

"You remembered? I do have the late shift on Sunday. But at least I'll have most of the day. I'll take you to lunch," Ms. Thompson said.

"It'll be your birthday, Mom. Let me take you out... Do you want me to make you some tea?" CJ offered.

"Could you baby? That would be nice. I like the way you change the subject," Ms. Thompson smiled.

"It's already decided. I got you," CJ said flashing a smile.

"Are you leaving soon, dear?"

"Yeah Mom, in about ten minutes," CJ answered heading to the kitchen.

His mother sitting with her feet soaking started to channel surf. "I still got time to catch 'The View'. I like that Star Jones." Ms. Thompson directed her attention back to surfing.

**11:25 a.m.**

James was sitting in the living room playing video games, still lingering over breakfast. Claudine's petite frame was fully dressed for work with only her shoes left to put on. She stared at James as she bit into a piece of toast and grabbed her pocketbook.

"Are you going job hunting today?" she asked.

James, uncomfortable with the question, put the game on pause.

"Why you ask?" he asked gruffly.

"Nothing, I just wanted to know if you were going job hunting today," Claudine answered, carefully measuring her tone.

"I have a lot to do in the house today. I don't know yet," James said solemnly.

As she turned to walk away, James heard a frustrated sigh escaping Claudine's lips.

"Claudine, hold up... What do you think? I don't want to find a job?"

"No one said anything about you not wanting to find a job. It's just—"

"You think it's easy, but I haven't had a steady job in two years. You think I like that shit?"

"Don't curse at me, James. I was just asking…"

"No you weren't just asking. I hate when you do that. If you've got something on your mind, why don't you just say it?" James exclaimed, walking around with his arms flailing.

Claudine stared at him trying to figure out what had gone wrong between them. Recently they seemed to be constantly at each other's throat. James paused and waited for an answer.

"All I'm saying James is you're an intelligent man and, yes, two years is a long time. Maybe you're not applying yourself the way you should," Claudine said, trying to be as delicate as possible.

Despite her efforts, James' wrinkled brow was clear indication that they weren't on the same page.

Claudine gently continued, as she tried to prevent the situation from exploding, "If you're hitting the market three days a week, maybe you should hit it four or five. Try doubling the number of resumes you send out."

James was in front of her nodding his head. A sardonic grin clung to the corner of his lips. His arms were folded as he looked her up and down.

"My, my how easy it must be for you to say that to me from where you're standing. I'm sorry, babe. But I'm not as cute as you are."

"Hold it right there. What are you insinuating, James? I…"

"What I'm saying is, I don't have the luxury of wearing my hair down with a miniskirt and some pumps," James said waving his arm as he described her attire. Claudine's mouth was agape. He continued, "I can't flaunt cleavage, smelling like sun-ripened raspberries and - boom- get a job." James wagged his finger from side to side.

"No, no, hold up. Fuck you, James! I work hard for everything I've got! Don't tell me…"

"Hey listen, I'm not knocking you. But let's keep it real here. I know the sisters don't have it easy. But an attractive woman with a degree will never ever have to struggle to get a job, so long as she wants one. Let's be real, Claudine!"

Claudine bit her tongue and the resulting silence reverberated through the entire apartment.

After a few seconds, James said loudly, "When I got laid off, the economy was already jacked up. How was I to know terrorists was gonna drop the bomb on us, right here in New York…?"

Another uncomfortable silence ensued. Claudine didn't want the situation to escalate further. Pondering their future, her fears came fast like her heartbeat, loud like the beating of drums.

**11:45 a.m.**

Actually, the sound of West African drums was coming from the apartment below. The vibe bounced off Fatima's earth-toned walls. She was seated crossed-legged on a rug in her living room. African art decorated the spacious room and a variety of plants captured her essence. Fatima, elegant with long, agile limbs, sat with eyes closed and appeared to be in a deep trance.

Her boyfriend Reggie, a young handsome African-American man was rushing to get dressed for work. He hurried into the kitchen, fiddling with his shirt. Fatima completed her yoga practice amidst the smell of raindrop scented incense. Reggie dashed into the living room, tucking his shirt in with one hand and eating a bagel sandwich with the other.

"Hey baby, I see you found your breakfast okay," Fatima smiled.

"Yes, thank you, baby. Look, I got to be out of here. I should be back from work around seven, alright?" Reggie said still multi-tasking.

"Okay, honey, have a good day at work," Fatima said giving Reggie a kiss.

Reggie grabbed his bag and was almost out the door when

Fatima called out to him.

"Oh honey, listen, before I forget, I made reservations for us tonight at the Jazz Lounge to celebrate your promotion," Fatima said walking to Reggie. "I want to take my man out tonight and show him how proud I am," she said wrapping her arms around his neck.

A big smile crossed Reggie's face. For a moment Reggie appeared to be speechless. He kissed Fatima passionately on her lips.

"I must have done something really good in my past life to luck up with something special like your fine-ass self. You go, my Nubian princess."

She was floored by Reggie's barrage of compliments. Fatima smiled and blushed like it was her first kiss. Butterflies were loose in her stomach and her knees were getting weak.

"Get out of here," she said recovering and playfully waving him off. "Go to work."

"I'll see you later tonight," Reggie said.

"Bye."

11:50 a.m.

Reggie blew her a kiss and was out the door in a hurry. He started down the stairs then suddenly seemed to change his mind.

Reggie checked his watch. It was 11:50 a.m. and he headed back upstairs. Tiptoeing past his own door, he dashed up another flight of stairs and quietly knocked on the apartment door directly above Fatima's.

Next door he heard the angry voices of Claudine and James reaching into the hallway. The floodgate of emotions had opened and Reggie could clearly hear the lovers' quarrel. He shook his head and knocked softly on the door.

"What took you so long?" said a voluptuous young woman, answering the door. "I thought you weren't coming to see me anymore," she continued, pulling Reggie by his collar inside the dark apartment.

"Uh uh, baby, you crazy? Come on now, Shay-Shay, how long you've known me?" Reggie asked putting his arm around her waist.

She pulled him close and their lips locked in passion. He closed the door to the heated argument lingering in the hall and threw his briefcase on the sofa.

Reggie had noticed Shay-Shay since they were teens. Both had grown up in East Flatbush. Shay-Shay dated other guys but she always had a thing for Reggie, as he did for her. Shay-Shay was well-proportioned, tall and brown skinned. She supported herself by dancing in the strip clubs of Manhattan and the Bronx. Often when Reggie claimed that he was with his boys, he was really in the club watching his favorite stripper.

He had been to her apartment before, but not in the past six months. His relationship was working out well with Fatima and Reggie didn't want to do anything that might mess it up. A couple nights ago he and his boys were celebrating his promotion. They wound up at a strip club in Manhattan and there she was, Shay-Shay on stage shaking her ass. His hunger for her body drove him to her apartment that day.

When it came to sex, Fatima was good at what she did for him. But Shay-Shay got down and dirty. After seeing her at the club, Reggie spent nights thinking of freaking off with her. Even though he had promised himself not to do it anymore, he couldn't stay away. Now Shay-Shay was working her show below his belt and his thoughts went blank. Reggie's knees buckled when her warm moist mouth engulfed him. He felt her tongue and his wall of morality collapsed. Relishing the sucking sounds coming from her lips, Reggie knew her brain game was intense.

**12:00 p.m.**

Claudine and James were locked in such a boiling conversation that steam was threatening to come off both of them. She had done everything to reduce the tension, but now felt she had to respond.

"I really don't know where this thing about me having suppressed thoughts is coming from. You of all people should know I don't hold my tongue. Maybe what you're going through is your own self-doubt," she said, arms folded.

"Why is it that a sister thinks she can analyze a motherfucker cuz she took a semester of psychology? Time out. It's all business with you. Everyday all you do is be on the computer and shit. How about me, man? What's up with some support?"

"How about you...? All you do is play Xbox all day, James! I mean c'mon, you're not in junior high anymore."

"First of all, your mother plays Xbox. Second, it's the only way I seem to be able to release any tension these days."

"Oh, and that's another thing. This thing about me not supporting you, brother, let me tell you, you're being supported every month! I'm sorry if I don't pat you on the back daily for trying to get a job, something you're suppose to be doing in the first place! I'm sorry, James, but when I get home from work, I'm not thinking about giving you backrubs. I'm thinking about making sure that all the bills are paid for the month. I mean, damn! How many roles do you want me to play, James?"

"I never asked you to play more than your role. I never asked you to be the man. You took on that job yourself. All of a sudden now I haven't contributed, right?"

"I didn't say that—" Claudine started but James interrupted.

"Look, I wasn't put here to be anybody's burden. Maybe I should just leave so you don't have to be so stressed out anymore," he said gravely.

"Hey, if that's how you feel, if that's what you want to do, I can't stop you."

The argument had gone too far this time. They both felt that there would be no turning back. Claudine looked at the floor as her tears rolled down her face. James turned his head to the ceiling. They were waiting for the other to give in, but it seemed that they had arrived at a stalemate.

"I'll start packing my bags this afternoon. By the time you get back from work, I'll return your keys to you and that's it," James said with conviction.

Deep down in the pit of her stomach, Claudine was hurting. Instead of showing it, she pulled out a compact case and checked her makeup in the mirror.

"Okay, fine, no problem...I have to go. I guess I'll see you when I get back...?" She asked, nonchalantly slipping the makeup case into her Coach bag.

"Yeah, alright," James said looking up at the ceiling. He heard the door close as Claudine walked out of his life with poise.

| BlacKout

# FOUR

12:30 p.m.

The barbershop was jumping with excited customers. The music videos continued to pump on BET and the place was abuzz with customers swapping the latest on current politics, money and women. L leaned against his booth reading the newspaper.

Outside, people were checking out Tech's wares. A customer walked up and gave Tech dap. Claudine went by and all eyes watched her.

"I'd go for her, one hun'red. Ah, but too bad she's damn-near married..." Tech said shaking his head. He turned to one of his regulars, "What up, Ty? You copped that latest Nas yet?"

"Yeah, you know, that nigga is the hottest in the game. I got all his shit," Ty answered giving a pound to Tech before entering the barbershop.

"My dude, you want a cut? I'm free..." L said greeting Ty.

"Yeah, you gonna stay free too if you waiting to cut me," Ty replied before finding a seat. Everyone in the barbershop cracked up.

"It's like that Ty? Oh ahight, I thought you was my man and all. You can't see a brother trying to eat, huh? You wanna play me? Cool. It won't be like this forever. I'm going hard body with my solo CD."

"Oh yeah, what it do?" Corey asked.

"It dropped this summer. Sixteen hot joints for five dollars, y'all! Tech's pushing'em hard body. Go ahead fellas, buy one now and I'll even sign it," L bragged.

He pulled out his CD, *The World According To L*. On the cover was a photo of him, desperately trying to achieve a menacing look.

"What it do? Lemme see," Corey said.

"When the majors see how many units I push for dolo, they gonna come knocking hard on my door. Then we'll see who sweating who?" L laughed handing the CD to Corey.

Raucous laughter spread around the barbershop. From his seat in the barbershop, Ty waved L off.

"Be easy. Don't harass my customers. You can't fault a man for not wanting to walk around with bald spots on his head," Nelson joked, as others joined in the laughter. He continued, "Dig this, y'all. I saw in the paper today that 50 percent of all Black males in New York City are unemployed. You believe that shit?"

"Fifty percent...?" Rick repeated.

"Fifty percent...? What you saying? The system is going hard body against the Black man?" L asked.

"That means more chicks for me, rookie. That's what's up. Ya know y'all dudes' trifling," Cam said, laughing by herself.

"It's a staggering figure is what it is. I don't know if I even want to believe it, you feel me? Let's think about it seriously. Are they counting the dollar van drivers out there? Are they counting people like Tech and the vendors on the strip, the self-employed? Did you file your taxes at the end of the year, Rick?"

"Huh...? I'm sayin, you working for the feds or sump'n?" Rick asked.

"Just do the math, man. We gotta establish our businesses. We gotta go from survival mode to developmental mode. We've gotta help and support each other. You feeling me?" Nelson said.

"What it do?" Corey asked befuddled, scratching his head.

"I'm saying we gotta stop depending on the—"

The conversation was abruptly interrupted when the door opened loudly. Rasheed, the neighborhood stick-up kid, swaggered into the shop and the place became deadly silent. Freshly released from his bid up north, he had a gangsta's rep and was heavy into illegal street antics. Rasheed surveyed the place before nodding at Nelson.

"What up?" he asked curtly, hands on his waist, as if he was sizing up the place.

All eyes were on him without looking directly in his grill. Rasheed's face was knitted tightly and he paced back and forth like a caged animal. He seemed to relish the rush that came with being feared by all. When Nelson acknowledged him with a nod, Rasheed ignored him and pointed at Rick like he had a gun in his hand.

"How many heads you got in front of me?" he barked, staring Rick down like there was beef between them.

"Two..." Rick answered raising his index and middle fingers. He seemed to be waving a peace sign.

"Hold my spot, ahight. I'll be back," Rasheed said. He walked out of the barbershop and arrogantly strutted down the block.

"Did y'all see the way he was creeping in here though? Ra's the illest stick-up kid on the block. Watch your shop hard body, Nel. That nigga touched," L said.

"His life's like an egg, wait a second and see how long it's gonna take them cops to crack it and do what they do," Corey said sitting nervously in the barber's chair.

"All I'm gonna say is this, that right there is some low-level, juvenile stunt. I'm a grown-ass man, fam. Don't step in another league you're not ready for, you feel me?" Nelson chuckled.

Everyone in the barbershop mumbled in agreement. They knew the reputation Rasheed carved out for himself throughout the neighborhood. He was the kid parents told their sons to stay away from. In and out of jail since his thirteenth birthday, he had done every crime from petty larceny to aggravated assault with a deadly weapon. Most recently, Rasheed served time for attempted murder in connection with a robbery. After he was released from an upstate lock-up, Rasheed was back on the block. Always on the hunt for a criminal enterprise, he recruited kids by instilling terror. He was the neighborhood bully and all the weak kids were his prey.

His swagger down the block proved it. Rasheed grabbed a handful of a young girl's ass as he headed down the street. Tech watched him and shook his head before walking into the barbershop.

"It is hot out there and I'm not talking only about the weather, one hun'red," Tech said.

"I didn't know they let Rasheed out. He on some criminal minded stuntin', hard body," L opined.

"I'm sayin', he been out like three weeks now," Rick said.

"Have you ever wondered why they release the grimiest Negroes in the summertime?" Nelson asked.

"Summer-recess," Rick noted. "Watch what I'm sayin'. He'll be back in before the summer ends. He's gonna be taking a few others with him too," he deadpanned.

There was an abrupt rumbling and commotion at the door, announcing the arrival of an old man with a dried up Afro and missing front teeth. Walking into the barbershop, pushing a shopping cart filled with junk and humming Sam Cook's *A Change Is Gonna Come,* this bum was on a roll.

"...*I was born by the river in a little tent, and just like that river, I've been running ever since... It's been a long time coming but I know a change is gonna come...*"

The old school melody came in a scratchy baritone soaked in too much alcohol and cigarettes.

"What's going on, fellas?" he greeted his listeners with the butt of a cigarette seemingly fastened to the corner of his mouth.

"Toothless Tone, wha' I told you about bringing that raggedy-ass cart up in my barbershop?" Nelson shouted in an already annoyed tone.

"Ah c'mon now, young blood, I'm trying to hook you up. I got some stuff for you on sale. Look, look, check this out..." Toothless Tone walked over to the nearest outlet and struggled with an old vacuum cleaner attached to a long hose. "Now, check this out. This here is a for-real Hoover classic. Your sweeping days are ova, playa. This thing sucks up everything in sight. And I'm selling it today for only fifty bucks."

"Forget it. Get out of here," Nelson said.

"Ha, ha, I'm just messing with you, my man. Gimme five dollars and you can have it. Look, I'll give you a little demonstration,"

Toothless Tone said plugging the vacuum in an outlet. "Now, check this out," Toothless Tone shouted turning the switch on.

Suddenly there was a loud explosion like a car backfiring. Customers jumped out of the barber chairs, taking cover from a dusty cloud of smoke.

"I'm sayin', what da fuck is this shit!" Rick yelled.

"If that's Rasheed, you better chill, hard body..." L said looking around.

Smoke from the old vacuum cleaner quickly enveloped the barbershop. Tech watched the proceedings in wide-eyed surprise from outside. People ran out of the barber shop fanning their noses and coughing.

"What da hell...?"

"I'm sayin' damn Toothless Tone, what is up with you, man?" Rick asked looking baffled.

"Toothless Tone for real, get da hell out of my shop and don't bring your ass back up in here no more. For fucking real, man. Get your fucking ass outta here...!" Nelson yelled.

"Nel, I'm sorry man look, I'll get it fixed and come right back," Toothless Tone said.

"No, don't come back! You're gonna scare all my customers away," Nelson shouted looking upset. "People get scared when you come around. Get that shit outta here!"

"Alright, fine. Have it your way. I'm out… You got a dollar?"

"No, I don't have a dollar. You gonna shove that shit up your vein!" Nelson shouted.

"How 'bout you, Rick?" Toothless Tone stopped and asked.

"We gonna be losing business because of you and now you want a dollar from me. Man, I'm sayin', get your ass outta here and don't come back!" Rick shouted.

All the customers shouted at Toothless Tone as he went around trying to drum up more business. Tech grabbed him by the collar and shooed him away. Customers and barbers alike were standing outside waiting for the smoke to clear.

"Anybody got a buck?" Toothless Tone asked and kept walking.

Toothless Tone was in his early fifties and most people believed he was missing a screw or two in his head. He had a stellar career in the U.S. Marines, receiving several medals for bravery, but returned from the Vietnam War with too many emotional scars. Over a period of time Tone lost not only his job but also his family. These losses, and his diminishing emotional stability, sent him down a road of homelessness and dereliction.

He pushed his cart and stopped when he saw three rappers approaching and heard their popping lyrics. He stood clapping, stomping his heels and smiling.

*They say it's its own planet...Ladies and Gentlemen... Welcome to Brooklyn...Bed-stuy Brooklyn New York...yeaaaaah...*

"Yeah give me some o' that good ol' freestyle, Chen Lo..." Toothless Tone hollered.

The rapper known as Chen Lo smiled and kicked lyrics so hard that Toothless Tone and the others who were hanging outside the barbershop started hopping.

*I take the A train home to BK*
*I'm a Brooklyn transplant by way of PA*
*Born in LA where they say its fantasy living,*
*superficial and surface*
*New York City Urban Transit is under the surface*
*where rats lurk*
*Crooked ass cops can random search us*
*This 9/11 shit has authorities claiming nervous*
*The Stuy is no different its Pigs all on the corner*
*A blatant occupation fam they trying to remove us*
*Most black are still renting...Jews are all the owners*
*These Koreans getting money...Arab and Latin*
*bodegas*
*I'm here...breathing dirty air*
*Garbage and shit is everywhere*
*It's not for the weak or the timid...you get ya*
*swagger here*
*Where hustle's the sport... "NEWPORT, NEWPORT"*
*Where Kane, B.I.G., Jay and BlackStar got a start*
*In the summer see the elders playing chess in the*
*park*
*Those who fell victim, inspiring murals of art*
*African and Caribbean cultures are mainstays*
*Everybody flaggin' 24-7 like "JUVE"/*
*It's Brooklyn...Better known as Crooklyn*

*Bedford and Fulton*
*Halal food from the Muslims*
*Flatbush, Crown Heights, Brownsville, Bushwick*
*BK to most Medina to the Five-Percent*
*Signing off with your Brooklyn report*
*Small slice day in the life here in Brooklyn, New York…*
*It's called Brooklyn…*

"Yeah, I feel you, my young brother," Toothless Tone laughed. "Hold on, before your man, what's his name?"

"I'm D-A-M-A-J-A-D," the other rapper spelled his moniker rhythmically.

"Yeah, before Damaja D spit, I wanna tell you something. You are the future. You got what it takes, Chen Lo. Make it happen and don't forget where you came from."

"Yo, Toothless Tone, shuddafuckup and let the young brother spit!" Tech shouted.

Fiery lyrics drew the crowd from the barbershop. Like moths to a flame they gathered to hear more from the young rappers. Toothless Tone, in the midst of the happenings, was still running his game.

"Yeah, yeah, I don't normally listen to rap but give me a dollar, and I'll listen some more, ha, ha," Toothless Tone laughed.

"That was some good advice, pop. I think it's worth a buck," Chen Lo pulled out a dollar and gave it to Toothless Tone.

"Alright, go on, lift these hungry black souls high with your lyrical gift, Damaja D," Toothless Tone said, smiling giddily as Damaja

D kicked his lyrics.

> Yo it's the reason why I fear less than average
> The reason why every bar that I spit do damage
> The reason for the tilt in my hat, strength in my dap
> Or why you might hear a little pain when I rap
> It's a fact
> I was raised by the city…no offense Mom
> Surrounded by grime and the gritty, you could see it
> when I ditty bop
> At a young age got used to sound of gunshots
> And now I see the hood for what it's worth and what
> it birthed
> It's the land of the free and the home of the brave
> Or should I say land of the lost and the home of
> slaves
> Could even say land of the G's and homes are their
> graves
> But never say land of the weak or the home of the
> fake
> Save face muh'fucka…round here we move at a fast
> pace and age at a mass rate
> Shit I'm a hundred and eight
> But all jokes aside you could see the fire in my
> eyes…
> I ain't lying for my home, I'll ride
> I'm from Brooklyn

"Ah yeah, ah yeah…before you go into the other verse, give me another dollar. I'll introduce you my young brother. "What's your name?" Toothless Tone asked.

"They call me Mo Betta Blues," the third rapper answered confidently.

"Blues…? Ah yes, that's my kinda thing…give fifty cents and

I'll introduce you," Toothless Tone smiled.

"Yo Tone man, why don't you let the brother kick his verse, one hun'red, c'mon man," Tech shouted.

"I'm just making sure this young brother gets his full props…" Toothless Tone started but Mo Betta Blues interrupted.

"I don't need no intro. Here's two quarters, ol' timer. I got this."

> The pistols is poppin the pumpers is clocking
> The haters is watching
> They waiting and plottn'
> This ain't Mr. Rogers neighborhood partner
> They'll stick Santa Claus for his stocking
> That type of beef don't come with a topping
> Its Brooklyn/Get you a big shirt Yankee fitted, rocked them Air Force Ones way before Nelly did it
> Around here when you talk it then you better live it
> It's that 718, that 187 district/where cops is crooked as a seesaw
> So squeeze first my hood definition of peace talk
> The streets talk and the cells whisper
> Cross that bridge shit it even smell different
> Inhale the gritty and the grimy, been a lot of places but it's really what's inside me
> Tatted on my arm you know exactly where to find me
> Trust you couldn't get a better picture from Spike Lee… It's Brooklyn…yeah… it's Brooklyn.

"Ahh yeah, that's some off-da-easy shit… One hun'red. What y'all say the name of that joint was?" Tech asked.

"Brooklyn…" the rappers chorused.

"Yeah that's fire…I got some new shit too," L added.

"Word…?"

"Let me hear sump'n then…" one of the rappers said to L.

"Yo, I gotta spark some o' that la la then I'll be ready hard body," L smiled.

"Y'all down with a manager…?" Tech queried. "Cuz you know—"

"Yeah, no digga, we down with John Hill, ya know? The album's fire! It's called *Chronicles of a Rebel* and will be out real soon…" the rappers answered stomping their feet with swagger. "It's gonna burn up the charts!"

"My joint is already out hard body, and I'm movin' mad units for dolo."

"Word…?"

"Word up. My joint is gonna do so well, BET is gonna have to give me an award so I can hang it over my toilet bowl, so when I'm shittin', I'll know that I'm the shit."

"I hear you L," Chen Lo said, laughing.

"Come check my CD in the barbershop…" L started then changed his mind. "You know what, the barbershop is like smoked-up so we better go on over here and blaze some trees…" L laughed, pulling out the blunt he had been stashing.

# FIVE

1:00 p.m.

CJ was in his bedroom getting dressed for his summer gig at Sneaker World, the local athletic shoe and clothing store around the corner. His shift started from two-thirty and ended at seven-thirty when the store closed. CJ sat on the edge of his bed contemplating what color sneaks went best with his new Cleveland Cavaliers Lebron James jersey. He decided on the ankle-cut, fresh white Uptowns and finished dressing.

The doorbell rang and CJ rushed to answer it. He opened the door and his best friend Ty walked in. The boys used to attend the same high school but when his parents divorced, Ty's behavior became erratic and he dropped out.

"What up, Ty?" CJ greeted.

"Chilling, man, just came from the barbershop," Ty said.

"I hear you. How's it out there?"

"It's hot like a... Yo, Chen and 'em niggas were out the block, spitting fire like God, son."

"Yeah, they be doing their thing."

"Yo, I'm feeling that Lebron jersey, kid. It's kinda hot," Ty said touching the jersey.

"Oh thanks, this just dropped like two weeks ago."

"I gots to cop me a pair o' them joints right there, CJ. You gotta hook me up with the discount, son. When you going to work again?"

"I'm headed out there in few. I'm just going out front to chill and get some fresh air."

"Is that Ty, I hear?" Ms. Thompson asked coming from her bedroom.

"Yes, Ms. Thompson. How're you doing?"

"I'm just fine, my boy. I hear you talking about sneakers and all that..."

"I wasn't talking 'bout no sneakers, it was his Lebron—"

"Okay, basketball...I just want to know when are you gonna go back to school and graduate, Ty? You used to do so well in school and when I didn't see you at the graduation, I was too shocked. What're you gonna do? Run the streets?"

"Nope, I'm gonna go back to school. I just gotta get my head together, Ms. Thompson."

"Don't take forever, young man. Time waits for no man."

"You right, Ms. Thompson, you are. I'll go back soon."

"I just hope so, Ty. Too many young black men are wasting their lives, too busy doing nothing."

"Yo, you ready to go?" CJ asked rescuing his friend from his mother's barrage.

"Yeah... Gotta be going now. So long, Ms. Thompson," Ty said quickly, walking out.

"Bye, Ty, come again. Take care, CJ," Ms. Thompson said kissing her son on his cheek. "Be good," she said locking the door.

The teenage boys walked out of the building. CJ was looking fresh and clean in the afternoon sun. Ty was sporting a fresh haircut and denim shorts with a white T and Uptowns.

"CJ, son your Moms be trippin' dogs. She blew my fucking high," Ty said.

"Yo, you still smoking weed? I thought you said you were gonna stop, Ty?"

"I took a few puffs with L earlier, but that shit won't last after your Moms, son," Ty said.

"Whateva, man, you do what you wanna do. I ain't the one who's gonna wind up working up in the back of Burger King," CJ said sarcastically.

There was a pause as Ty stared at the busy sidewalk of Flatbush Avenue. He swallowed hard before saying anything.

"Yo, why you always dissing me, son? I mean, why you had to go and tell your mother that I had dropped out, huh? School ain't for everyone, you know? And if I'm feeling like dropping out, so be it. That's my fucking biz! You gotta go snitch, so you can look good, son."

"Yo, you got it twisted. I didn't tell my mother that to look good. She ain't seen you at graduation and she asked me what happened. What? Was I gonna lie to my mother? No," CJ said leaning against a parked Bronco. "Yo, just stop making shit so personal and try to straighten out your life."

"That's the same shit you told me when I told you how honey had dissed me, son."

"Diss you when? What honey, Ty?"

"You remember that light-skin shortie, Paula. She liked me and you told her I was working at Burger King. She never talked to me again."

"Yeah, and didn't she went and get pregnant for a damn drug dealer?"

"Yeah, but she was fine and all that, and she could've been mine," Ty said reflecting.

"Ty, you didn't need all that stress she would've brought you. She wanted everything bling-bling."

"Yeah, she was kinda gold-digga. But why people can't give me a break the way they do with you? Everyone be actin' like they know what's wrong with my ass. Everyone should just leave me da fuck alone! Why can't people just get da fuck off my tip, son?"

"Cuz you ain't me, that's why. I'm suave, intelligent and debonair, my man" CJ boasted.

"You right, I'm walking around under a black cloud. But you still ain't had to tell your Mom," Ty said leaning against the side of the truck next to CJ.

They continued looking up and down the block. A small group of teen girls walked up and flocked around the two boys. Ty loved the attention and eyed a pretty teenage girl. He pulled her along with him to the corner store. CJ saw Ms. Germaine approaching the building lugging two bags filled with groceries.

"Hey, Ms Germaine," CJ greeted the elderly woman.

"Hey CJ, how are you?" she smiled.

"I'm fine. Let me help you with that," CJ said taking the bags from her.

"Oh no, baby, it's okay. I don't want to trouble you. You're hanging out with your friends and all. I'm sure you've got things to do," Ms. Germaine said struggling to carry the bags.

"Here let me take those for you. It's no trouble at all," CJ said taking the bags effortlessly.

"Thank you so much, baby. You go ahead and leave them in front of my door. I'll only slow you down."

"Alright, Ms. Germaine," CJ said disappearing inside the

building. On the way back out he passed Ms. Germaine on the first stairwell.

"Thank you, CJ," she said, breathing hard.

"Not a problem, Ms. Germaine, anytime," CJ said and posted up against a car parked in front of the building.

Behind him another teen was moving in quickly, catching CJ unawares. Ty jumped on CJ, playfully taking him down on the hood of the car.

"What now, nigga?"

"Get the hell off me, man!" CJ yelled, struggling to free himself.

Ty started laughing and held CJ in a chokehold, locking him in brotherly love. The two friends laughed heartily.

"You crazy, Ty."

"Fam, I told you I'd bag that shortie. Got her number right here," Ty bragged, hugging CJ.

"Ty? What you doing, kid? She was only talking to you because I wasn't around."

The two friends were chit-chatting when the pretty young teen walked passed them and crossed the street. Her eyes were immediately locked on CJ's every move. Ty looked on in dismay as she blew CJ a kiss. He wanted the same type of affection that the neighborhood chicks showed CJ.

"Hi, CJ," she crooned seductively.

"Hey, what up, ma?" CJ casually replied.

"You tell me…" the young girl smiled flirtingly.

"You know, just maintaining…" CJ answered.

"You look like you doing a lot more than that," she said.

"You're looking real nice, ma," CJ complimented.

The teen girl walked away with an extra swing of her hips, smiling from ear to ear. Ty shook his head in amazement.

"So now, Keisha acts like she don't even see anyone else," Ty said in mock seriousness. He smiled as he imitated her, "'Hi, CJ!' 'What up, ma?' I don't believe shortie dissed me like that after giving me her number!"

"Don't hate, dog," CJ joked.

"Yo, I'm hit that before you leave for school," Ty laughed.

"Yeah, sure you are…"

"I got her digits right here," Ty said.

"That's probably 1-800-dial-a-joke or sump'n," CJ laughed. "I got all these young honeys on lock, son. I told you when you stay in school—"

"Ahight yo, I already heard that preaching shit from your Mom," Ty cut in.

He saw Khalil walking down the block toward them with some goons in tow. Ty's demeanor transformed immediately to street grit. Rasheed lagged way behind. Ty lit a Black and Mild and started puffing.

He then pulled out a Dutchmaster and split it open. CJ watched with wide-eyed surprise as Ty reached into his pocket and came up with a dime bag of weed.

"You ain't planning on doing that in front of my building, are you Ty?" CJ asked frowning. He felt his heart beat increasing.

"Yo, it seems like we right on time," Khalil shouted with his eyes on Ty.

Ty stared for a beat at CJ without answering. He turned and smiled at Khalil. CJ, Ty and Khalil were once childhood friends who would argue over everything from fashion to girls to music. But since Rasheed's release from an upstate penitentiary, they had chosen separate paths. Khalil was down with Rasheed. As soon as the thug returned home from doing his bid, Khalil quit school and linked up with him. Now it seemed Ty was also getting in with their thug plan.

"What up, what up?" Ty greeted with street swagger. CJ observed Ty thugging up as Rasheed got closer. "What's good, Rah?"

"What's up?" Rasheed said, mean mugging.

CJ easily greeted Khalil but seemed uneasy when it came to Rasheed. He barely looked at the thug when he said, "What up, Rah?" and nodded uncomfortably.

Rasheed looked him up and down. Then without speaking, he gave CJ a terse nod. Every time they met, Ty, CJ and Khalil engaged in a conversation about the hottest rapper or the best basketball player, the same way they used to when they were in school.

"Hove's the best out there," Khalil said before launching into a Jay Z freestyle.

"*I'm so far ahead of my time, I'm about to start another life / look behind you I'm about to pass you twice / back to future I gotta slow up for the present/ I'm so fast niggas can't get pass my past / how you proposed to deal with the perfect present when I unwrapped the gift and curse in one session?*"

"No, c'mon man Nas is da realest..." Ty insisted and jumped into a verse of Nas rhyme.

"*I've been fucked over, left for dead, dissed and forgotten / Luck ran out, they hoped that I'd be gone, stiff and rotten / Y'all just piss on me, shit on me, spit on my grave / Talk about me laugh behind my back but in my face / Y'all some well-wishers, friendly actin, envy hidin' snakes / With your hands out for my money, man, how much can I take?*"

"I'm saying Nas Escobar," CJ said siding with Ty. Then they both burst into more Nas lyrics from *Ether*.

"*When these streets keep callin, heard it when I was sleepin / That this Gay-Z and Cockafella Records wanted beef / Started cockin up my weapon, slowly loadin up this ammo/ To explode it on a camel, and his soldiers, I can handle / This for dolo and it's manuscript, just sound stupid...*"

They laughed, then CJ and Ty sprayed Khalil with some more Nas' lyrics for a grand finale.

"*When KRS already made an album called Blueprint / First, Biggie's ya man, then you got the nerve to say that you better than Big/ Dick suckin lips, why ain't ya let the late, great veteran live…*"

"Oh shit," Ty shouted, "that's my shit right there, son." He laughed embracing CJ with a pound and glad handing. They continued rapping and spitting lyrics together.

"*In '88 you was gettin' chased through your building / Callin' my crib and I ain't even give you my numbers / All I did was give you a style for you to run with / Smilin' in my face, glad to break bread with the god / Wearin' Jaz chains, no tecs, no cash, no cars / No jail bars Jigga, no pies, no case/ Just Hawaiian shirts, hangin' with little Chase / You a fan, a phony, a fake, a pussy, a Stan / I still whip your ass, you thirty-six in a karate class / You Tae-Bo hoe, tryna' work it out, you tryna' get brolic? Ask me if I'm tryna' kick knowledge / Nah, I'm tryna' kick the shit you need to learn though / That ether, that shit that make your soul burn slow / Is he Dame Diddy, Dame Daddy or Dame Dummy? / Oh, I get it, you Biggie and he's Puffy.*"

"Ooh, he killed that. Nas killed it with that Ether," CJ said. He and Ty laughed, hugged while sharing more daps.

"Ah man, he ain't done numbers like Hova did yet. Look how long da nigga's been in the game," Khalil said dissing.

"Exactly, and he keeps doing it. He'll get his," CJ shot back.

CJ, Ty and Khalil continued to yuck it up, but not Rasheed. He remained quiet and spent the time eyeballing CJ's gears and jewelry. Rasheed seemed to be scheming on the diamond-encrusted watch and the long chain hanging at CJ's waist.

"Fuck both 'em niggas! They both wack! Ain't but one king of rap," Rasheed said. "And that muthafucka's dead."

"Yeah, you right, Rah. Both of them fell off bad lately..." Ty agreed. He seemed to hang on to Rasheed's every word.

CJ looked at Ty with surprise written on his face. Ty couldn't even speak his own mind. It was clear that his best friend was doing all he could to stay on the good side of Rasheed. CJ watched Ty put the blunt between his ear and his Yankee Fitted.

"I thought you were gonna light that blunt already, nigga?" Khalil asked.

"Nah, nah, I'm a spark it in a few," Ty answered smirking at CJ.

"I hear you," Khalil said smiling and nodding.

"Gimmie da blunt, nigga," Rasheed demanded.

Ty pulled the blunt out and handed it to Rasheed, who stuck it between his lips as he spoke.

"Yo, how I look just standing here with this swagger-jacking-ass nigga? Let's push over to da 'Bush and check out some fine-ass birds. And we can get some of these packs off," Rasheed said standing with what seemed like the butt of a gun sticking out of his waistband.

"No doubt," Khalil and another crony immediately agreed.

"Yo, y'all rollin'?" Khalil asked.

"Nah, I'm chilling. I gotta go to work," CJ said.

Rasheed looked over at CJ with disgust. Khalil looked at Ty. Ty seemed conflicted, glancing back and forth as if nervous about making a decision for himself.

"What you doin', Ty?" Khalil asked.

Ty hesitated for a beat and glanced at CJ. He saw the frown CJ bore and was about to answer Khalil but CJ interrupted.

"You need to fall back," CJ blurted staring at Ty.

"Nah, nah I'm good…" Ty said hesitating.

"I know this scurred-ass nigga ain't opening his mouth to me?" Rasheed asked glaring at CJ. "My strap will put a stop to all that yak," he continued, sneering at CJ and tugging at his waistband.

"No, it's all good. He talking to me," Ty calmly said to the angered Rasheed.

"Whatever, man. I'm out," he said waving off Ty.

"Ahight, later," Khalil said exchanging daps with CJ and Ty.

They all walked down the block. Ty kept puffing on a cigar. He wanted the type of rep that Rasheed had gained, but also the respect of the neighborhood. As soon as Rasheed came back to the block, Ty started hanging with the career criminal.

"When did you start smoking weed, hanging with niggas, getting off packs, Ty? You really need to fall back, son. It seems like I don't even know you no more."

Ty continued puffing on the Black and Mild cigar. Looking around, he saw a black Lincoln turning on to the block.

"That's Sol's car. He owns a couple of the buildings around here," he said changing the subject.

"I've lived around here all my life. I know Sol," CJ said looking at Ty. "It's you I'm trying to figure out."

"You know when Sol comes around, sump'n major is always about to go down. He never be around to fix them buildings, yet," Ty said turning his head to look at the car. CJ stared at him.

Sol was a Jewish man in his mid-forties. Stern and business-oriented, he was the landlord of three buildings on Browser Street. He was with his driver and assistant Tony, a blue-collar Italian in his mid-thirties.

It was 1:15 p.m. when Sol's car came to a stop in front of 254 Browser Street. Sol sat in the car holding a clipboard and going over his schedule for the day with Tony.

"You know we've been getting a lot of complaints, particularly with the Browser buildings. To be honest with you, Sol, I don't think George is doing such a good job maintaining them anymore," Tony said.

"That's exactly why I'm here. We're gonna pay our friend a visit. Do an inspection and get some comments from the tenants. If I don't like what I hear, he's gone. He's been in that apartment for about thirty-two years now. I can fix up the apartment and double the rent," Sol said with a smirk.

"Sounds like a plan to me," Tony said nodding his head.

"I'm so happy you approve," Sol said sarcastically.

# SIX

**1:20 p.m. 254 Browser Street, Brooklyn**

James was in the apartment cleaning up. He took out the garbage, made the bed, and swept the living room. Then he laid flat on his back on the floor, clearly upset about the argument he and Claudine had earlier. He plopped down on the sofa, bored and exhausted. He turned on the television in time to see a commercial.

*"...If you're still experiencing difficulty sleeping, having panic attacks, or are depressed as a direct result of the events surrounding 9/11 please give us a call. Our counselors are experienced in dealing with post-traumatic stress..."*

The ad jarred James' memory and sent him reeling back to that fateful morning of September 11, 2001.

*James, clean cut and nattily dressed in a pin-striped suit, was on his way to work. He had just gotten off the subway at the Wall Street station. James stepped into the chaos that took more than 3,000 lives. He watched with the crowd in disbelief as the plane* crashed into the tower of the World Trade Center, then pandemonium broke lose. The plane collided violently with the columns immediately below James' office.

"Oh my God," James screamed, running toward the building.

People watched in horror as workers jumped from their building. Falling from so high up, they never stood a chance. Police and EMS were beginning to evacuate the site. As he took off running, his cellphone rang. It was Claudine frantically screaming, trying to find out if he was okay. He was sobbing when he answered.

"Baby, it's crazy out here but I'm alright. I know...my train was delayed...any other day I would've been up there already... I don't believe this," James' voice cracked with emotion. "My coworkers, my friends, they were all up there..."

James picked up the phone and dialed the hotline.

"Hello," he said. "I was involved in 9/11 and I was wondering if you could help me...?"

**1:25 p.m. Manhattan**

The *Uptown* magazine office was abuzz with young, energetic people running to and fro, trying to meet the latest deadline. Claudine appeared busy at her computer but was distracted and barely able to maintain her composure. Unable to hold it together, she burst out in tears. Embarrassed, she pulled a tissue out of her desk drawer and dried her eyes. Dedra, her best friend, noticed and walked to her desk.

"Hey girl, what's wrong?"

Dedra pulled up a chair and sat next to her. The tears and frown were stark changes from Claudine's normal sunny disposition.

"Ah, Dee, me and James had a nasty fight this morning. I think we're breaking up. He's moving out today," Claudine sniffed.

"Are you serious? Wow, I'm sorry to hear that. What happened?" Dedra asked worriedly.

"I can't even remember how it got so serious. I was pissed off at him for not waking me up for work this morning. I asked him if he was going job hunting today. Then he just went off on me," Claudine said with a lot of emotion.

"Why didn't he wake you up?" Dedra asked, intensely curious at this point.

"Huh? Oh, he was going to surprise me with breakfast in bed."

"That bum. You need to drop him fast, girl."

"Stop it, Dedra. That's not funny. You know I take my job seriously. You know how hard I worked to get this promotion."

"First of all, you're one of the few people here who are allowed to work out of their homes. Take advantage of it," Dedra said.

"Yeah, but sometimes I just can't concentrate at home and I don't want to neglect my job," Claudine said.

"Nobody's telling you to neglect your job. But you sure better not let it make you neglect your man," Dedra cautioned.

"I don't think I'm neglecting James," Claudine retorted.

"I wish I could find myself a good man who cares about us spending enough time together. Your ass was probably up all night writing, right?" Dedra asked. Claudine nodded. Dedra gave her a knowing smile and continued. "Mmm, mmm, mmm, you involved chicks kill me. You've been out of the singles arena for too long. Ain't nothing out here, girl."

"This isn't about being single or with someone else. I'm not checking for anyone," Claudine said defiantly.

"So then, what's the problem?"

"I think we're both getting frustrated with our financial problems over the past year," Claudine said with concern.

"Let me tell you something, Claudine. Jobs, finances, they come and go. I've always admired your relationship with James. It would be a shame to see that fall apart, over stuff you two have no control over."

Claudine thought about what Dedra said for a beat. She hugged Dedra as tears streamed down.

"I gotta go, Claudine," Dedra said. She got up and pushed the chair back in to place. "Are you going to be alright?"

"I'll be fine. Thanks, honey," Claudine said reaching for more tissue.

"That's my girl," Dedra said winking as she walked away.

"Now, I can't wait to get home." Claudine smiled.

"Don't forget that staff meeting at four," Dedra reminded Claudine. "But I know you just can't wait to make up now," she laughed and disappeared down the hall.

# SEVEN

2:00 p.m. Brooklyn

Sun-drenched Flatbush Avenue was teeming with pedestrians. Vendors selling ice-cold bottled water were having a field day. Back on Browser Street, a reckless young man roared down the street on his motorbike and popped a wheelie to everyone's delight.

"I gotta get to work, Ty," CJ said walking away.

"I'll walk with you," Ty said following CJ.

CJ seemed to be in deep thought , until he finally spoke.

"Ty, why do you act like that around Rasheed?"

"What're you talking about, CJ?"

"I'm talking about you acting like you scared. You be acting real funny. You start acting differently whenever that nigga comes around. Everything he says, you agree with. What's up with that?"

"Yo son, it's like this, I'm not going away to college. Truth be told, I may never leave da muthafucking 'Bush 'cept in a body bag."

"So you're gonna let someone have you living in fear for the rest of your life?" CJ asked.

"What da fuck am I 'sposed to do, son?" Ty asked.

"Try growing up and being your own man. That would be a good place to start," CJ said getting closer to Ty's mug.

"Yeah, that's cool but I still gotta live here," Ty said holding his ground.

"That doesn't mean you gotta be a knucklehead!"

CJ and Ty stood toe to toe. They were so close they could smell each other's breath.

"You can go ahead and be different and all. But muthafuckas will make your life real miserable. Sometimes you've gotta accept life for what it is. You know what I mean? My father walked out on my Mom and her whole life turned upside down. She had to accept that," Ty said turning and walking away.

"For real, Ty? You can't be serious," CJ said shaking his head and catching up. "You have to stop making excuses and feeling sorry for yourself, Ty. Grow up!"

The lifelong friends walked by the front of the barbershop. Customers and barbers were still outside waiting for the smoke fumes and dust to clear out.

"Yo, what da fuck! This a strike or sump'n?" Ty asked laughing.

"You ain't funny," Rick said.

"What's poppin' my dude?" L asked.

"What up L? Is we gonna hit up some la...la-la, la, la tonight?"

Ty sang.

"If you buying, why not? For real, you got dough, right?" L replied smiling.

"Damn, CJ! That Lebron James jersey is what's up, kid," Cam gushed.

"Good-looking-out...I'll holla at y'all later. I gotta bounce," CJ said exchanging daps and walking away.

"Ahight, Mr. Penn State," Nelson hollered after him.

Across the street, a chubby, eight year old boy stuck his head out the fire escape. It was Cam's younger brother.

"Hey Camille...! Yo Camille!" a young voice called out.

She looked up at the boy with daggers in her eyes. If looks could kill, he'd have immediately fallen off the fire escape. Cam ran across the street chased by raucous laughter echoing loudly behind her. Her family was not impressed that Cam -though she was a very pretty girl- seemed to need to dress like a man.

Camille came out as "Cam" to the rest of the neighborhood when she was a senior in high school. She hung with the fellas, and it wasn't long before she was a regular of the barbershop crew.

"What the hell is it that got you calling me out like that?" Cam shouted at her younger brother.

"Mommy wants you to buy her a pack of Newports," the kid yelled from the fire escape.

"Tell her to give me the money. That's what's up."

Her baby brother threw down a crumpled paper towel with change and some bills wrapped in it.

"Tell her this ain't enough. What am I suppose to do with this?"

"Mommy said for you to figure it out, Camille."

"Listen to me you little fuck-face. How many times do I have to I tell you not to call me by my home name when I'm in the streets? Don't let it happen again," Cam stated irately.

"Yeah, yeah," her brother said waving her off.

Cam stomped off to the bodega. Ali was standing outside and she whisked by him. He was about to follow her into the store but glimpsed Fatima. Ali seemed enamored as he paused to hold the door for her.

"Thank you, Ali. How're you doing?"

Ali's eyes followed Fatima's every move, smiling shyly when she caught him staring. He stood by the door trying to play it cool, but it was clear that he yearned for this beautiful young woman.

Cam bought the pack of Newport's and greeted Fatima as she walked out of the store. Ali's eyes followed Fatima around the store as she picked up fruits and vegetables. She walked to the counter and waited while the clerk tended to another customer playing Lotto.

Ali became furious when the clerk kept Fatima waiting. He

shouted angrily in Arabic then apologized to Fatima for the clerk's indiscretion.

"I try to explain to him, 'Always serve the customers with groceries first', but he does it wrong anyway. I'm sorry Fatima," Ali said.

"It's all good, Ali. I can wait. It's not a problem," Fatima smiled at Ali. His eyes smiled back.

"No really, you deserve -you demand- that kind of attention. You're a strong, decisive queen who knows what she wants. Therefore, if there's something that she asks of me, surely, I cannot front," Ali responded rhythmically.

"What...? Let me find out that you got a flow. That was really cute. You got some skills, Ali," Fatima smiled.

Though proud, he made a face at the woman purchasing Lotto tickets. She had been staring and snickered at him.

"You know, since I heard you perform, I've been dabbling in a little poetry during my spare time. When is your next show?"

"Actually tonight, I'm taking my man out to the Jazz Lounge and afterward I'm going up to perform a song and a surprise poem for him," Fatima said with more excitement than she intended.

Ali's face fell to ground level. It dawned on him that he may never have a chance with the object of his desire.

"How nice," he said, shielding his disappointment.

"I'll see you later, thanks," Fatima said, walking out the store.

"Bye, Fatima," Ali said. "Lucky Reggie," he whispered below his breath.

**2:10 p.m.**

Reggie and Shay-Shay were on their backs in her bedroom. After a heated lovemaking session, their naked bodies were covered with perspiration. They lay breathing in the bliss. Shay-Shay puffed on a cigarette.

"Damn girl, you put it on a brother," Reggie said wiping sweat from his face.

Feeling gassed, she suddenly jumped on top of him. Shay-Shay's hands gently tightened around his neck as she spoke.

"I know you don't think you coming here to give me just one round, right?"

"Ma, I'm a heavyweight. Don't come at me like that," Reggie countered.

She rolled off and walked to the bathroom. A few minutes later she came out dressed in cut-off denim shorts and white wife-beater.

"I'm going to the store and get some munchies. You want anything?" Shay-Shay asked.

"I'm good," Reggie said.

"You got any change?" she asked, walking out of the bedroom.

"Yeah, check my pockets."

"Ahight, oh, by the way when I get back, you better be ready," Shay-Shay warned.

"Damn! I should've drunk some Tiger Bone, today," Reggie whispered to himself.

He peered at his watch, yawned and rolled over. Reggie closed his eyes and drifted off to sleep. Shay-Shay locked the door and started down the stairs.

2:15 p.m.

Browser Street was hot and bothered. CJ and Ty walked side by side to the sneaker store.

"I'm a holla at you later," CJ said giving Ty a pound.

"I'm gonna come by later and check out what I want you to pick up for me. Cool…?" Ty asked.

"I got ya. What you about to get into?" CJ asked.

"Nothing, just chill," Ty said.

"Yo, stay out of trouble," CJ said.

"No doubt, son," Ty said with a smile.

CJ glanced at his watch and disappeared inside the busy sneaker store. There was a crowd of shoppers checking out the neighborhood's largest collection of sneakers and athletic gear in style. Mr. Yoon, a Korean man in his forties and the owner, was at the cash register, while his wife, in her late thirties, and their son, Billy, assisted customers.

The family had owned the store for fifty years. The sneaker and clothing store was started by Mr. Yoon's father who grew up on Browser Street. The family had relocated to Long Island ten years ago but the sneaker store, owned by the family, remained a cornerstone in the neighborhood.

"Good afternoon, Mr. Yoon," CJ said walking in.

"Hey CJ, it's a little busier than expected today. Let's do the inventory later. Please help Billy with the customers."

"No problem, Mr. Yoon," CJ answered and headed to where a group of people stood admiring the new Jordans. "How're you doing today? Those are crazy-nice. What size would you like those in? You're gonna love them," CJ said, walking away.

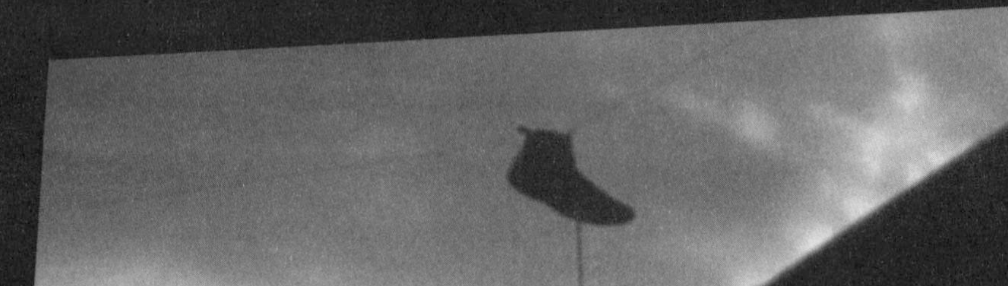

# EIGHT

**2:20 p.m.**

Fatima came up to the building as Shay-Shay was leaving for the store. They gave each other cold stares for a beat. Shay-Shay snickered as she sashayed by. Fatima stopped, turned around and watched in bewilderment as Shay-Shay laughed while walking down the block.

Fatima was aware that Shay-Shay knew Reggie. About a year ago, they had all met at the Jazz Lounge. A mutual friend introduced her to Reggie and Shay-Shay. He and his boys were there one night when she was performing in the spoken word segment. From there, they started kicking it. She remembered the evening so well. Fatima spent a few minutes thinking and sighed. Their chemistry was good from the jump. It must have been the romantic poetry of Osekre, the Ghanaian poet. Fatima smiled as the verses of *You Are* softly resonated in her mind.

*Sit down*
*And come around*
*Close your eyes*
*And see the light*
*Tie your tongue*
*And sing aloud*
*Don't walk*
*Let your feet do the talk*

*When you threw me out of the deep*
*Into the winds*
*To find the stints*
*And re-define the limits,*

*When you showed me new heights*
*And opened my heart with your insights*

*I went around the world…*

*Flying knowing I couldn't glide without your backing*
*Trying, discovering I couldn't slide without your*
*standing*
*I was dying realizing I could die in your rising*
*I flew because I died to the fears that held you and I*

*I can't stop thinking about you*
*Or talking about your beau*

*I sit to view*
*And think of you*
*And wish to let you know…*

*You are…*

*You are… my wings*
*And my feelings*
*The meaning*
*Of my vision*

*You in my wings*
*Has become a disease*
*I tolerate with ease*

*You in my wings*
*Has become my reasoning*
*And unbelief*

*It's startling…*

*Because of you*
*I am trying to find the balance*
*In my misunderstanding*

*The stirring*
*In my distraction is disturbing*

*Because you are all I have been discerning–you are*
*confusing my learning and yearning*

*You are constructive*
*Labeled as destructive*

*Cohesive*
*Posing as adhesive*

*You are my understanding*
*Posing as distressing*

*Affectionate*
*Pretending as impassionate*

*Caring*
*But seem to be eluding*

*You are forgiving*
*But never believing*

*You…*
*You are*
*Trying to make me dislike you*

*Turning me against myself*

*Making me enemy of me*

*See…*

*My heart is on your side*
*And my mind is on my side*

*My thoughts are for me*
*But my words elude me each time I speak to you…*

*You*

*You are…*

*Making me re-write*
*My dreams*

*Sampling them*
*Before I sleep*

*Tasting the alphabets I assemble before I speak*

*I am forming sentences without construction*

*Ha…ah…ah…ah…ha…*

*I catch myself thinking about you*
*I stop myself from trying to see through you; trying not*
*to take another look at you*

*I wonder*

*…Why you?*

*But who are you?*

*Your spirit is a reflection of something daunting*
*Forming in my passion*
*-Less haunting*

*Aiding a confusion*
*Which I have no way of understanding*

It seemed just like yesterday that Reggie and Fatima became more than just good friends. Six months after they started dating, he was having problems at his former address. She asked him if he wanted to move in with her, as she needed someone to share the rent. She neglected to tell him that it was really that she needed him near. The truth was she had completely fallen for Reggie's charm.

He was always great company, kind and very respectful to her, but it seemed his friends were resentful of her. Being more spiritually inclined, Fatima didn't hang out with them drinking. She also noticed that ever since Reggie moved in with her, Shay-Shay, who lived upstairs, had been throwing shade. Their interaction went from smiling and saying hello, to just nodding politely, to not even looking at each other. Now Shay-Shay was openly scoffing at her.

It was 2:25 p.m. when Fatima wearing a soft smile, walked back to the building. She opened the door to her second floor apartment and put down all the groceries inside the kitchen. Maybe she would fix Reggie his favorite chicken dinner. She walked to the bathroom and stood in front of the mirror.

She took a deep look at herself before raising her blouse and loosening her bra. Fatima examined her naked breasts for several minutes. Cuddling and fixing her nipples, she glanced at herself from various angles. She slowly wiggled out of jeans and looked at her shapely thighs. Pulling down her panties, she patted her taut stomach. Fatima twisted her body to stare at the roundness of her derrière. A confident smile unfurled. She threw a kiss at her mirror image, "I'm gonna knock Reggie out tonight," she smiled and softly whispered the words to another Osekre poem.

*See?*

*You've triggered my energy to attention*
*You've compelled my senses and tenses*
*To strive for a compilation of information*
*To decipher*
*The stanzas*
*And find the answers*
*That connects you and I*

*You are a positive*
*I cannot understand*

*Meant to fit into my negative*

*Our magnetics*
*Holds the concentric*

*Pulls the eccentrics*
*And results in the dramatics*

*Here I am*

*Looking at you from the temple of my imagination*

*Thirsting to drink from the brooks in you*

*Waiting to hold your smile in the hands of my*
*thoughts*

*To shake your hands*
*Even if they will pour out like sands*

*To hear your story*
*The story with which you came to this mountain*

*To carry your dreams*
*Dreams of you*
*In baskets*
*On streams*

*To feel your fires*
*As I try to see through your eyes*

*You… you…*

*Are…*

*…my fear and my fire*

*I think of you*
*And I shudder.*

Her heart came alive reciting the rhythmic verses of the gifted African poet. It brought Fatima back to the time when Reggie and she first met.

"I think I'll do that number for my Reggie again, later," Fatima whispered aloud.

It was 2:27 p.m., when Sol got out of his car and leaned against the passenger door. Looking up at the building, he turned to his driver.

"Listen, this is what I want you to do. I'm going to find George and check the place over with him. To save time, I want you to carry out the rest of the day's schedule," Sol said looking at his watch. "It shouldn't take you that long. So be back around four-thirty and get me."

"You sure you want to stay out here by yourself, boss? I mean I can stay with you and double the workload tomorrow. It's really no big deal," Tony said.

"No, don't you worry, I'll be fine. Just be back at four-thirty," Sol said turning to walk away.

"Whatever you say, boss. I'll be right out front at four-thirty," Tony said.

"I'll see you then," Sol said tapping the rear of the car.

The car took off as Sol walked up the steps to the building. There were children playing in front the building and the three West Indian women were seated to the side.

"What's this...? We have a barbecue going on out here today?" Sol asked sarcastically. "Okay kids, let's clear the front, please!" he shouted.

Fearing the repercussions, Sol did not look at the West Indian women directly when he spoke. Instead he passed them and then looked back with disdain. They greeted him with disgust written all over their faces.

"Next time that rich mon look pon mi like that again, mi a go bust him upside the head, you know!" Beatrice said.

Shay-Shay strutted by the barbershop on her way back home. All the fellas standing in front stared at her rotating hips and her rotund behind.

"Ooh, she's off the charts. I'd love to crush that," one of them said throwing a kiss.

"Ah yes, I'd eat that up. Yummy," another customer said biting his fist.

"Shortie got it one hun'red. If I hit that, her nigga ain't getting her back, man," Tech said shaking his head. "Buy a CD from me," he said handing his next customer a CD.

Shay-Shay was an around-the-way girl who clearly enjoyed the attention. The fellas watched her hips twisting more as she flaunted her assets, sashaying down the street.

"Double damn!" someone shouted after her.

Shay-Shay walked back into the building and saw Sol knocking on the super's door on the first floor.

"You gotta knock louder. The super's probably sleeping," she smiled, going up the stairs seductively.

"Thank you," Sol said watching her shapely legs and round ass continuing up the stairs. "Thanks," Sol mumbled, biting his lips and returned to knocking on the super's door. Moments later, George answered the door.

"Sol, this is a surprise," George said opening the door. "I wasn't expecting to see you. Were we supposed to be having a meeting today? I didn't get the—"

"No, we weren't," Sol said cutting him off and smirking.

Without waiting to be invited inside, Sol brushed past George and squeezed his way into the apartment. He stood in the middle of what should've been a living room. The one-bedroom apartment was cluttered with tool boxes and used spare parts. The furniture inside the apartment was old and broken. Work clothes were strewn all over the place.

"I hope I didn't disturb you. You weren't sleeping or anything like that, were you?"

"Now why would I be sleeping in the middle of the day?"

"I'm going to be straight with you, George. I've been receiving several complaints about you regarding keeping up the building. And it's starting to be a problem. I'm concerned that perhaps you're getting too old, and I may have to get a replacement for you," Sol said.

George looked as if the building had just fallen down. He looked around the room and back at Sol.

"If this were to happen, unfortunately I would have to remove you from this apartment."

"I've been in this building for over thirty years. And I've been the super for nearly twenty years. Now if you want to get rid of me as a scapegoat then you go right on ahead. You ain't fooling nobody. I'm not stupid Mr. Berman. I know what you're doing."

"Now hold up, George. I think we're getting a bit ahead of ourselves here. That's why I came down personally, to look at the condition of the building with you. We can talk to the tenants and make an assessment. I'd like to get started and after that you and I can come back here and discuss the matter."

"If that's what you wish. Hey, you're the boss," George said following Sol out the door.

**◄ ONE WAY**

2:30 p.m.

Shay-Shay locked the door to her darkened apartment. Everything was quiet and all she heard was soft breathing. She walked over to the bed. Reggie was lying on his stomach wearing only boxers. She stood over him admiring his muscular frame before wiggling out of her shorts.

"I guess you didn't understand me when I said I wanted more," she said peeling off her top.

Reggie rolled on his back but didn't respond. He was asleep.

"This nigga gonna give me some more, if I have to resuscitate his ass." Shay-Shay smiled, gently pulling on him. She put him in her mouth and began sucking, deep-throat, snaking her tongue.

After a few minutes, Reggie opened his eyes and a big smile creased the sides of his mouth.

"Ah yeah, baby-girl, you do that so well."

"You love my skills, huh?" she asked pouring kisses on Reggie while her fingers roamed next to his brown-wrinkle.

"No, no," Reggie cautioned, as she got too close for comfort. "Don't do that."

"That woke you up, huh?"

"That shit turns you on? Well, you giving me brains turns me on," he laughed, shoving her head down.

She continued sucking until Reggie was ready to explode.

"Oh shit, baby, don't stop now," Reggie screamed holding her ears.

"Ooh, I don't wanna swallow your kids. Let me ride it," Shay-Shay said straddling him. She smiled and pulled him closer. "Ah Reggie..." she sighed when she felt him. Shay-Shay was rocking back and forth, riding as Reggie quickly recovered. Reaching up, he started massaging her breasts.

"Oh yes, Reggie," she moaned.

"I told you I was a heavyweight," he grunted.

Sweat poured off her brown skin as Shay-Shay's head snapped back. Reggie thrust his hips upward and she started to go wild. "Oh yes, baby. Give it to me." Shay-Shay was in ecstasy.

He flipped her off, and her mouth latched onto him like steel on magnet. Shay-Shay gobbled him up, making him disappear down her throat. She licked him all over and Reggie wailed like a newborn baby. He couldn't take it anymore and was about to explode. He rolled her over, doggie style.

"It's getting hot in here," he said after some long hard strokes. Reggie wiped the sweat off his forehead and slapped her naked, perspiring, round ass. Their sexual romp intensified with each hard stroke.  "Take this," he grunted, sweating.

"Give it to me harder, Reggie," she whimpered in pleasure.

Reggie's fingers traced the slut marks tattooed on her lower back.

"Oh, yesss…!" Shay-Shay screamed in sinful delight.

It was sexual liaisons like this that both tortured Reggie's mind and kept him up nights wanting her.  Shay-Shay was any man's fantasy when she danced, and he dug the way other customers in the strip clubs drooled over her.

"Yesss!" Reggie hissed blissfully when he reached her warm mouth.  Her coiling tongue brought him out.

# NINE

3:00 p.m.

All the smoke and dust had finally cleared up and everything returned to normal inside the barbershop. Customers were back in chairs and barbers were finishing up haircuts. L flipped through the pages of a newspaper.

"Yo, you think Kobe did it, man?" L asked looking up.

"Did what? I'm sayin'," Rick said.

"Nah, my man's wife's too fine for him to be doing that shit," Cam said.

"What's that they say? Show me a gorgeous woman and I'll show you a man who's tired of hitting that ass, you feeling me?" Nelson laughed.

"Kobe ain't raped no one, man. I'm sayin, he's got too much to lose. That cat can have any chick he wants. He don't need to go raping anyone," Rick opined looking around for anyone who was in agreement with his view.

"Including a white girl?" Cam asked with sarcasm.

"Oh boy, here we go again. Now the woman in you wants to come out, huh?" Nelson opined. Cam waited for him to continue. "Every time something like this goes down there's always a sister around to bring up the white girl issue. Get outta here with that! It ain't just the white girls. Let's not forget what they did to Mike," Nelson reminded all.

The customers and some of the barbers nodded in agreement. They all seemed caught up lamenting the fate of the former heavyweight champion.

"Or Pac, I'm sayin', God bless the dead," Rick added and everyone again nodded.

"I guess we're two for two, hard body. Let's not forget about O.J." L interrupted the spell.

"Hell naah," someone shouted amidst the chorus of boos that came streaming out of everyone in the barbershop.

"Getting back to Kobe, ain't his wife white anyway...?" L asked with a chuckle.

"No stupid, she's Dominican!" Cam shouted triumphantly.

The entire barbershop broke down laughing as L struggled to find something to say.

"Oh, no wonder he bought her that expensive ring from Harry Winston. You know how'em Spanish women love jewelry? It be like: 'Baby who fuck you better? Go and get me an expensive piece or that's it…'" L started but Corey cut him off.

"Nah man, all women ain't like that. Here's what it do, the other day I messed up and bought my girl diamond earrings from out on da 'Bush…"

"Hold up, did you say diamond from da 'Bush…? You better double check. I ain't heard about no diamond being on da 'Bush, a good while now," Nelson chuckled.

"I'm sayin', if you value that relationship you better get her diamonds from Jake's in Manhattan," Rick said.

"Word, your girl could be walking around with some cubic zirconia, talkin' 'bout 'My man loves me so much'…" L mimicked and the whole barbershop cracked up.

"I'm sayin', the best place to go is the Jews, man," Rick opined. "That's how you know you gettin' the best standard in gold."

"Nah man, them Italians be hard body with it. They got some real good shit," L said. "They be taking that shit off the Jews like what!"

"Man, the Arabs got 'em all…that's really what's up," Cam said.

"The Arabs are about oil, hard body," L argued. "Yo, check out that phatty right there!" he exclaimed with a long whistle.

The whole barbershop became distracted by the swinging hips of another round-the-way chick walking down the block.

"Hmm… Latina power, that's what's up!" Cam exclaimed.

"Ah shit, don't tell me you're gonna start bringing up JLo and shit," Nelson laughed.

"Nah, she ain't gangsta enough for me…" The barbershop chorused on cue, laughing.

# TEN

**3:45 p.m.**

Across the way in nearby Hallsboro Projects, a small housing area on the edge of Flatbush Avenue, people went about their business as usual. Televisions and radios blared loudly outside the doorways of the residents. Fans and air conditioners hummed through the windows. Children ran around playing hopscotch. Out on Flatbush Ave customers were busy shopping in the stores.

**3:50 p.m.**

Over on Browser Street residents were outside when the super and Sol knocked on the door of a third-floor apartment. A few doors down the hallway, James was on the computer, job hunting. He heard screaming and banging coming from a bed next door. Then he heard moaning and finally quiet. James scratched his head and got back to his job search.

It was 3:57 p.m. and the heat had most people going in and out of the bodega, purchasing cold water and stocking up on their beers and juices.

CJ, assisting another customer in the sneaker store, ran up the stairs to retrieve the requested pair of Adidas.

WELCOME TO **BROOKLYN**

**4:00 p.m.**

In her downtown Manhattan office, Claudine sat in the weekly staff meeting taking notes, appearing to be listening intently. When her eyes met Dedra's, they exchanged knowing smiles. It was clear that Claudine couldn't wait to get home. The talk she had earlier with Dedra had given her a better perspective on what she should do. Claudine was already thinking about what she wanted to say to make James stay.

WELCOME TO **BROOKLYN**

**4:01 p.m.**

Inside the barbershop clippers were roaring and the sound of video music blasted on the television set.

The customers in the barbershop had their eyes on the T.V.

"Is that Ja Rule and Ashanti? Turn that up. I love that joint," L said reaching for the remote.

"The volume is all the way up already. You feel me? Are you going deaf or sump'n, man?" Nelson asked.

"You got jokes," L said pointing the remote and turning up the volume.

**4:02 p.m.**

Zap. The lights and sound went out and everyone in the barbershop trained their gaze on L, holding the remote.

"Now you done did it, L. I told you not to fuck with the damn remote!" Nelson said looking up from the customer in the chair.

**4:05 p.m.**

In ninety seconds a summer blackout hit over fifty million people on the East Coast and Midwest. Customers in this Brooklyn barbershop, however, were none the wiser.

"Word, didn't you hear the man," Cam joined in. "All you had to do was put down the remote, you rookie."

"It wasn't me," L said with the remote still in hand. "I ain't done nada, for real, dogs."

"Then what the fuck happened…?" Nelson pondered.

"Tell me, you ain't paid Con Ed? They don't play around. They'll turn your lights off, hard body," L quipped.

"You only did half my hair," the customer sitting in Nelson's chair said after couple seconds of eerie silence.

"You got me," Nelson said smiling. "Pay me half the price."

"This ain't funny," L said.

"I think power is off all over the projects. Look over there by the entrance to Hallsboro. Power is out, and that's one hun'red," Tech said walking inside.

**4:10 p.m.**

The entire barbershop emptied. People glanced down to the corner and saw there was no light in the bodega. Some of the customers started pressing on their cellphone buttons furiously, but to no avail.

"Them Arabs at the corner store must not have paid their bills either," Nelson observed.

**4:12 p.m.**

Inside the bodega, Ali watched the last customer leaving

store.

"Now what…?" he pondered aloud, picking up the phone. Ali listened for the dial tone. It was dead. He slammed it down and walked outside. Ali saw people running around and fire trucks racing by. He watched the chaos slowly developing.

By around 4:15, everything in New York City had frozen. There were elevators stuck between floors in the Hallsboro Projects and the people trapped inside screamed for help. A teenage girl kicking it on her cellphone abruptly lost connection and spun around to check her bearings. The residents of Browser Street stormed outside searching for answers. Sol and George came out of the building and the tenants immediately flocked to Sol.

"Mr. Landlord, what happened to mi electricity, heh?" Ms. Germaine asked in frustration.

Sol scratched his head and was about to respond. Before he could deliver an answer to the first question, other tenants jumped in the fray.

"Mr. Landlord, what the hell's going on…?"

"Now just wait a second here," Sol said raising his hand. "We checked our circuit breakers and it's not our fault. I think the power is off in the whole neighborhood. Now if you can relax for just a few minutes, I'll try to get to the bottom of this."

4:18 p.m.

James anxiously walked out of his apartment after attempting to use his telephone in vain. He encountered worried pedestrians bum-rushing the police on the beat, looking for answers. Even the cops were unaware that a power outage had enveloped the city, causing the greatest blackout in the nation's history.

A man carrying a battery-powered radio turned it up as the newsflash was being broadcast. Many people descended on him to hear the breaking news.

*"The entire city of New York is experiencing a major blackout. I repeat, the city of New York is experiencing a blackout. Con Ed is currently reporting that the power outage is in an early stage and believe the source of the problem originated as far off as Canada. They are currently working to return power to the local area. We'll keep you posted as events develop… The time is 20 minutes after four in the afternoon. This is your 24-hour news station…"*

Ali was still standing out front. He saw pedestrians fighting to board a bus. Police were rushing to direct traffic.

"Good thing this happened during the daytime," Ali said

whistling loudly.

**4:22 p.m.**

Around the corner at the electronic store customers were milling about outside. Inside, the Russian owner and four employees were contemplating their next move. The owner was nervously pacing back and forth, awaiting further news on the electrical power situation.

**4:23 p.m.**

There was a swift and violent crash, and an explosion of broken glass. People ducked for cover as the front window was smashed open. A gang of opportunists rushed the store and began ransacking the place. They grabbed computers, camcorders, videogames, players and television sets. The owner tried to prevent the looting, but a gang member knocked him down. The employees gave way to the onrush and looters started carrying off merchandise.

James saw mayhem going down inside the store and raced over. Inside, the owner was being trampled on the floor as people helped themselves to all kinds of electronic equipment. One of the employees tried to intervene but was met by a punch to the face.

Suddenly James collared the assailant and threw him to the floor.

"You don't work here, man!" The other looters ranted at James.

"What the fuck is wrong with y'all. Get out!" James replied with anger.

Some of the looters left the store immediately while others tried to test James. He was unyielding, throwing punches at the young thugs who were trying to rob the store. A tussle ensued and James held his ground fighting off some of the robbers. Eventually they ran outside and James helped the store owner to his feet.

"Thank you," he said. "I'll never forget your kindness, young man."

"Not a problem. Don't worry about it," James said walking out of the store.

Outside in the streets, complete bedlam had broken out and the rowdy crowd dispersed in disarray. The commotion had ambulances and emergency vehicles racing.

4:30 p.m.

The Yoon family, CJ and about three customers remained sequestered inside the sneaker store. The sounds of sirens blared loudly all around them as they waited for the power to be restored. Ty came running into the store, breathing hard and clearly hyped by the events.

"Son, you heard? There's a blackout in the entire city!" He shouted between breaths.

"Yo, I know, we heard the news report a few minutes ago. What's going on, outside?" CJ asked Ty.

"I don't even know. But the shit is bananas..." Ty said looking around the store. "Those Air Force Ones is hot, son."

4:35 p.m.

Mrs. Yoon let out a loud scream. All eyes turned to see what was wrong. Rasheed, Khalil and three other goons had bum-rushed the sneaker store. CJ jumped between them. There was a scuffle that pitted Ty against CJ.

"Nah yo, I can't let y'all do this!" CJ said grabbing Khalil.

"What you care? You acting like shit belong to you," Khalil said defiantly.

"It doesn't matter, I work here. It ain't right! C'mon, y'all got to bungee," CJ said, undeterred.

Mr. Yoon's son, Billy, tried to stop a member of the mob. One of the thugs swung and Billy ducked and hit him with a right hook. The thug fell and CJ pushed some looters out of the store. Mr. Yoon threw his body against some merchandise and held on for all his worth, but Rasheed's arms were filled with sweats, T-shirts and sneakers. CJ rolled up on him, yanking him by the arm.

"Yo Rah, what's up with that, man? What you doing?" CJ confronted him.

"Muthafucka, is you stupid?" Rasheed asked freeing up one of his arms. He shoved CJ with such force it knocked him over a bench.

Sirens became louder, the emergency vehicle got closer. Rasheed and his gang took off. Mr. Yoon helped a pissed-off CJ to his feet.

By 4:35 p.m. all the stores on Flatbush Avenue were closed. Owners rushed to pull the gates down to prevent further looting. Staff was sent home as the chaos continued.

**4:40 p.m.**

Ali and his co-worker were out front watching and waiting. Sirens were blasting and pedestrians crowded the streets trying to get home. Police were racing to the crime scene.

"We'll be fine," Ali said to his coworker. "Just bring the gate down halfway and sell through the opening. People are going to need food and water. There's no telling how long this is going to last," he said looking around. They lowered the gate.

Nelson, Rick, Tech, L and Cam sat outside the barbershop watching pedestrians racing everywhere. Some ran for buses that didn't stop and others for cabs that were speeding away filled to the max. Minivans and special buses got crowded as soon as they stopped.

"This shit gonna get a whole lot crazier, you feel me?" Nelson said.

"Oh yes indeed," Rick said. "I'm sayin', that's why I'm gonna get a Red Bull and Guinness and go see that shortie from Lincoln I was telling you about."

"You better get you some condoms too, the way you be making 'em babies, hard body," L chuckled as the others kept their eyes on what was going in the streets.

"Shit, you really better go hard. That might be the last piece o' pussy you get for awhile. You never know how tomorrow's gonna turn out," Nelson said.

"Word up, that's one hun'red," Tech agreed.

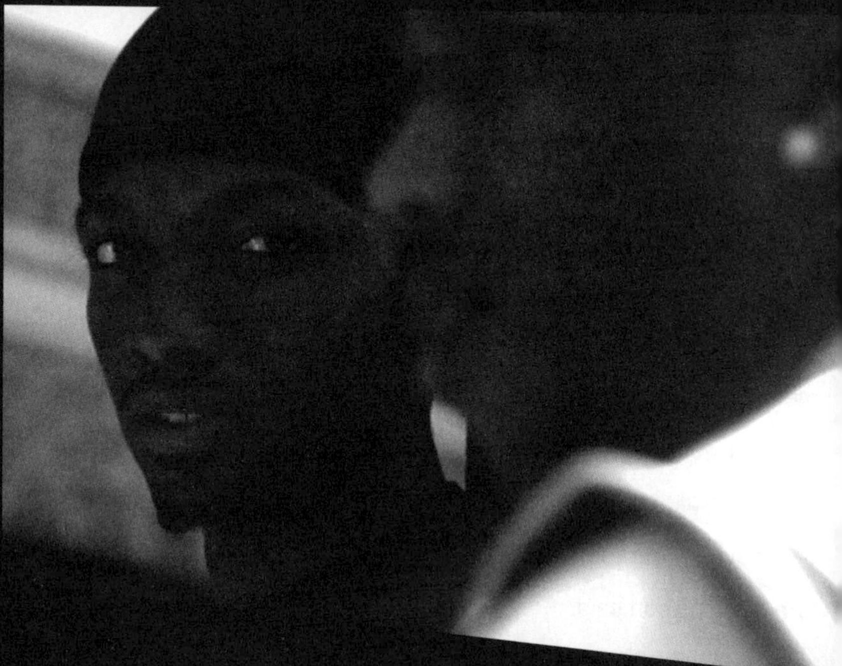

# ELEVEN

**4:45 p.m.**

CJ assisted Mr. Yoon with closing up the store. He accompanied the family to their car. CJ was very dismayed by what happened earlier in the store. When they reached the parked van, Mr. Yoon shook CJ's hand.

"Thanks, CJ. Please get home quickly. It's not safe," Mr. Yoon said.

"Ah, don't worry about me, Mr. Yoon. I live here. I'll be alright. You guys be safe traveling," CJ said waving.

The Yoon family got in the van and drove off. CJ started down the strip heading back to his block. Police in riot gear were out and some of the areas were blockaded by patrol cars. The crowd was disorderly, running behind the emergency vehicles. He smiled when he saw a group of preteens holding a makeshift sign that read, 'stop' as they tried to help police with the traffic on their block. CJ felt someone grab him from behind, spin him around and push him against the gate

"Hey man, get off me. What you doing, man...? Rasheed!"

"That's my word, if you ever put your hands on me again, nigga, I'm a murder your ass. You hear me?" Rasheed asked pressing CJ's back against the gate. CJ tried to resist but it was no use. "Did you hear me?"

"Yeah, I heard you," CJ shrugged.

"Pussy-ass-nigga...!" Rasheed spat, pushing CJ's face against the gate. "I'll smack the shit out you next time. You heard me? Pussy-nigga," Rasheed said as he walked away. CJ was left brushing his clothes off.

**5:00 p.m. Manhattan side of the Brooklyn Bridge**

Claudine and Dedra were among the waves of pedestrians trudging into Brooklyn. It was hot and humid, and throngs of people were crushed elbow to elbow as they made their way home. Frustrated, Claudine dialed on her cellphone with no success.

"Dammit! I can't get through. Let me try your cell," Claudine said to Dedra.

"Ain't no use trying, girl. I can't get any reception either," Dedra responded.

"Oh man, I was so hard on him today. I hope he didn't go job hunting after all. I heard on the radio earlier that thousands of people are trapped in the subway. Can you imagine that? I hate to think that James might be down there. He's asthmatic," Claudine said. They walked a few feet and were sweating. "Can you imagine how hot it is down there with all those crowds of people?" Claudine asked her mind solely on James.

"Relax, honey. Wherever he is, I'm sure he's fine. He'll make his way home like everyone else. The best thing you can do right now is go to the house and wait for him there," Dedra said.

"I guess I don't have any choice. How're you getting home?" Claudine asked.

"By foot if I have to. I'm just going to keep walking until I can find a cab or a dollar van or sump'n going uptown," Dedra said stopping. She looked around and saw people rushing back and forth. "Where there's a will there's a way," she said.

"Be careful and call me later," Claudine said hugging her.

"I'll see you tomorrow," Dedra said getting on queue for a dollar van.

Claudine continued walking over the Brooklyn Bridge with the many other New Yorkers stranded by the blackout. The dollar van left without Dedra. She hailed a cab and it pulled over with several people inside. They made room for her and drove off. Claudine soon found herself walking with a group in good spirits. They talked noisily, but when the topic came up of Al Qaeda possibly being responsible for the blackout, she could feel the fear rippling through the crowd. Pretty soon the conversation died and everyone focused on getting home safely.

WELCOME
TO
**BROOKLYN**

**6:00 p.m.**

Browser Street, Brooklyn was buzzing. People were everywhere talking loud and getting supplies from the bodega. Ali and his coworker were busy running to fill customers' orders. James was out on the street, his brow wrinkled with concern. He was pacing back and forth in front of the building frantically trying to reach Claudine on his cellphone.

"Damn!" he muttered under his breath.

James stopped pacing and looked around to see the police arresting looters, and he desperately wanted to be by Claudine's side. The morning had gone badly and now he wished they hadn't argued. All he wanted to do was to make sure she was alright. He whispered a silent prayer and walked back to the building.

The West Indian women were outside expounding on their

own theories about the blackout.

"Mi feel it in mi heart that Bin Laden has something to do with this, ya know?" Beatrice said beating her chest with conviction.

"You think so?" Sister Carol said, looking around.

Some residents were sitting on the stoop in front of the entrance. Others congregated at the side. Everyone seemed to have abandoned their homes. Sol and George walked out.

"Where the hell is my driver? He should've been here by now," Sol said looking up and down the block.

Standing at the entrance of the building, George held the door for someone rushing inside. Sol looked worried as he waited. There was no car.

"He's probably stuck in traffic," George reassured.

"That's a possibility, but he should've been back before all the craziness started," Sol said impatiently.

"Take it easy, Sol, he'll get here soon," George said.

"Easy, I'm going to ease my way out of this madness. Let's go to the corner. I'll catch a cab," Sol said.

George and Sol walked to the corner. A crowd was standing around chatting. They quieted down when the news came on.

"...The city is presently working with Con Edison to restore power before midnight. There is no cause for alarm. There has been no evidence whatsoever of terrorist involvement. In addition there *have been no report of violence or rioting…"*

"Riot…? When's the power coming back on? That's what I wanna know!" Someone shouted.

"B-o-o…"

WELCOME
TO
**BROOKLYN**

By 6:30 p.m. there was a long line snaking around the block to the pizza shop. People were preparing for the evening. The staff was busy throwing pies in the gas oven. Across the street, a long line developed in front of Ali's bodega. Toothless Tone walked the line harassing the customers, begging for change.

"This a damn shame, people…! Even on doomsday you can't find it in your heart to help your fellow man. That's exactly why it's about to get crazy. This is all a ploy by the government to kill the black man!" The crowd ignored Toothless Tone but he didn't stop. "That's right you heard me. They not gonna turn on so much as a light bulb until they find every last one of you niggedy negroes dead, on the floor like this…"

Toothless Tone threw himself to the ground flat on his back. Then he started twitching as if caught in the throes of death. The people on line laughed.

It was close to seven and George was still standing with Sol on the corner. They attempted to flag down cab after cab with no luck.

"This is utterly ridiculous. I can't believe none of these cabs are stopping," Sol said, sounding nervous. His whining attracted unwanted stares.

"Yeah, muthafucka, now you see how it feels to be treated like us. That shit doesn't feel too good, huh?" an onlooker shouted and the crowd roared.

"Okay, I think it's time for me to go," Sol said pulling George along.

"Maybe we should go back to my apartment until you can get a hold of your guy," George suggested.

"I think that's a very good idea," Sol said, walking quickly away.

They walked past Ty just as CJ was approaching him. CJ's frustration was obvious.

"What's up with you, Ty? Why you left me for self and took off like that?" CJ asked angrily.

"Shit, nigga, the law was coming," Ty answered.

"You see your mentality, dog? You didn't do anything, right? So why are you running from the police?" CJ said. He was in Ty's face but Ty was not retreating. He came back at CJ.

"I don't know bout you but when I hear po-po coming, I dip.

You go ahead and stand around while they sweeping people up. Any nigga will do! But I guess you don't have to worry about that kind of shit. Huh, Joe College…?"

"Yo Ty, dead that, ahight…? I'm tired of your fucking ghetto mentality. Don't run game on someone who's known you your whole life. Your dad was a lawyer, right? Stop following these goons, man for real, Ty. That shit ain't gonna lead to nothing," CJ said pushing on Ty's shoulder.

"C'mon man, we boys…" Ty said grabbing CJ's arms. CJ shook him off and walked away. "CJ, I'm a talk to you, man. It's all good," Ty said, watching him walk away.

CJ stopped and gave daps to James, who was still punching the keys on his cellphone.

"What's up, CJ?"

James walked to where all the fellas were standing outside the barbershop. He greeted the group, giving hugs and pounds.

"It's crazy out here, man," James said.

"Yeah, they wilding out here," Nelson concurred.

"For real, for real," James said.

"What…? They done ran up in the electronic store and the sneaker place. They robbed'em both," L said.

"These cats out here don't waste time, huh?" James said.

"What I'm not understanding is this. Why would you want to

loot a store in broad daylight just because there's a blackout? Doesn't that defeat the purpose?" Nelson asked scratching his head. "Am I the only one who don't get it?" he asked.

Everyone stopped and thought about the question Nelson posed.

"Word, it's like I see you, nigga. I know who you are and I'm gonna send the police to see you," L answered laughing.

"Yo James, is your girl good, man? I saw her going to work and I know she works in Manhattan," Tech said.

"I don't know. I just hope she's alright. I can't even reach her by phone. I'm just praying she isn't caught in an elevator or the subway... I'm a go down the block for a minute, though, so if y'all see her tell her I'll meet her at home," James said.

"Yeah, no doubt, I got you, fam," Tech said.

"We lucked up a little bit. I heard over at Hallsboro Projects they don't have no gas or water," L said, laughing.

Toothless Tone walked by the group outside the barbershop. He stopped and stared at them. "I told you they were gonna starve y'all niggas," he said.

"Oh they gonna be buck-wild over in the projects tonight. You can't even call 911," L said.

James headed back to the building and passed the man with a battery-powered radio. People gathered around listening to the news.

*With the streets flooded with people and many walking over the Brooklyn Bridge, the caller said he felt this was reminiscent of 9/11...*

"Can't nothing compare to 9/11," James said shaking his head.

# TWELVE

**6:45 p.m.**

In the rough and gritty housing projects known as Hallsboro, the blackout was the worst thing that could've happened. Residents had no running water, apartments were being robbed, and grocery stores were completely shut down. Nothing moved except the rats and roaches, and the low lives of the underworld, crawling around and setting traps.

Outside was for the brave at heart and those who were hard as rocks. One such group had gathered on the corner in front of the closed bodega. The grimiest ones were using the traffic light as a chin-up bar, including a muscular thug with a wide back. His tall, lurking frame was intimidating. Other street goons came through showing him respect with daps and fearful nods.

"What up, Wisdom?" one of the street goons shouted.

"That's right, nigga. My cousin home, yo. It's about to be

popping in a minute, dogs," the thug said as he finished his set.

Two ethnic African women wearing ceremonial garb walked toward them. It was clear they were afraid at the sight of the thugs. They began speaking in their native lingo and crossed the street to avoid any trouble.

Wisdom completed his set. Jumping down, he gave daps all around and joined his crew holding down the corner. Another soldier jumped up and started to work on his chin-ups. Wisdom strutted around, snarling and seemed to be itching for something to pop off. To the delight of his crew, Wisdom shadow-boxed for a minute.

"Yo Wisdom, you still got it. You's da muthafucking man," one of the goons shouted, clearly impressed.

"What da fuck! I should've stayed locked up north and shit. This some ol' Gaza strip shit! Muthafuckas ain't got no water, ain't got no stores to stick up. This ain't Africa, Ethiopia, Sudan, Iraq...they go through this same shit everyday. Having to kill another nigga in order to eat sump'n," Wisdom spat and the goons listened intently as he continued. "Let's walk over to the holy land. I bet y'all, stores are open there. I bet they got running water and fucking food! Shit, a nigga and his kids gotta eat. Like Robin Hood, I'm gonna have to take it and bring it back to my fam!" Wisdom declared.

His goons strutted away from the corner.

"Yeah, Wisdom, let's lay someone out," one said.

"I got my Four-Pound ready to run up in anyone clothes," another said.

"Yeah, we ready for this," another joined in.

It was close to 7:20 p.m. and all the residents were out on Browser Street. The hoods of cars were transformed into sofas and the happenings in the street were more interesting than any reality TV show. People were trying to remain cool. The long line continued outside Ali's bodega.

The sun faded, leaving the streets a dark hue. It was close to pitch black when residents realized this would be no ordinary evening on Browser Street.

"Smells like someone's barbecuing," Fatima said.

"They're doing everything out here," CJ said.

Fatima, CJ and friends from the building sat on the hood of a car chatting it up. Fatima seemed restless, checking her watch every few seconds and looking all around. After a while she shook her head.

"I'll see y'all in a few," Fatima said and quickly walked inside the building with a worried frown.

Reggie and his side-dish were spent and slept for some time. The place was in complete darkness but he could feel her arm and naked legs on him. He stirred, opening an eye and glancing at the clock. It was blank. Reggie looked at his watch.

"Oh shit!" he exclaimed jumping out of the bed.

"What's the matter?" Shay-Shay asked groggily and drifted back off to sleep without waiting for his answer.

"Oh damn! I gotta go right now. I'm late for..."

He was in too great a hurry even to wash. Reggie grabbed his bag and rushed out of the dark apartment. He scurried down the stairs, fixing his clothes along the way.

At about 7:27 p.m. an exhausted Claudine finally arrived on her block. She carefully waded through the sea of people. Some were drinking while others barbecued and partied. Having walked all the way from Manhattan, Claudine was sweating and tired. She came close to the building and saw CJ.

"Hey, Claudine," he greeted with a hug and kiss on the cheek.

"Hey, CJ, how's your mother?" Claudine asked, returning his kiss.

"She's fine," the teen replied.

"It's starting to get dark. You should get inside soon. Don't stay outside too late, alright," Claudine instructed.

"I won't," CJ said.

7:28 p.m.

Reggie opened the door to the apartment he and Fatima had been sharing for the past 2 years. For the first time, Fatima was waiting on him. As soon as he walked in, he could sense that something was wrong. Candles were lit and incense was burning but something wasn't right. Reggie hugged the woman he called a Nubian princess.

"Thank God, you made it home safely, baby," Fatima said greeting Reggie. She seemed anxious but was happy to see that he had made it home.

Reggie hugged her lightly but she pulled him close as if he had survived an alien attack. He held her smiling but Fatima wasn't letting go. Inside, he breathed a sigh of relief. She was happy he was home. Now they could go out and have fun like she had planned.

"No doubt, I was rushing. I didn't want to miss tonight's little celebration," Reggie said smiling and kissing her. "I know my Nubian princess got sump'n special for…"

"Hold up… rushing?" Fatima paused and pulled away.

"Yeah, c'mon I wouldn't miss it for anything. So I rushed home directly after getting off work. Let's freshen up and get dressed for this night out…"

"You did a full day's work and didn't have any problems getting home from work, Reggie?"

He could barely look in her eyes, and wanted to make it short.

"You know I always get to work, and why would I have a problem getting home?" Reggie asked. "Let's get dressed or we'll be late," he said walking away.

"How did you get home so quickly? I mean, I don't understand..."

Fatima's face seemed strained-- was it confusion or fear. Reggie smiled hoping to ease the mounting tension.

"Baby, I got home the same way I always come home. You

know, by the subway," he lied cautiously.

"How's that possible?" Fatima asked. Her darkened brow revealed that her curiosity and anger were rising.

Reggie felt the room closing in on him. There was nowhere to run. His awkward smile crept from his face. Her curiosity seemed to boil over into immediate anger. Her nostrils flared, daring him to say something else that would sink him even deeper into the quicksand of deceit.

He looked away in shame with his mind in an awful whirl. Spinning out of control, Reggie was cramming to understand her line of questioning. Shay-Shay could've told Fatima while she went to the store. He thought not. Reggie had known Shay-Shay too long for her to double-cross him.

"What do you mean? How's that possible?'" he asked, still unsure of what she was getting at.

"The trains haven't been running since four this afternoon, Reggie!"

Her words rang in his ears but weren't registering in his cranium. Not knowing what else to do, Reggie looked at her and shrugged.

"I really don't know what you're trying to say. Because I—"

"How did you get home by train, Reggie?" Fatima asked cutting him off.

"I, ah, I ah…I really had no problem catching my train," Reggie said, his lips had gone dry. He tried to change the subject. "Let's get ready for this thing…"

"What the hell was this train running on, Reggie? Batteries…? Power has been lost in the city since this afternoon."

He was really nervous now. His eyes opened wider than before. Sweat beads forming on his back and under his collar. The air seemed to have left the room. He sucked at the air as if he was having an asthma attack. He continued speaking shakily, barely able to move his lips. Reggie's thoughts overwhelmed him as he continued.

"Well…ah…I don't know maybe my train was a special train."

He tried to fake a smile but Fatima got closer to him and looked in his eyes. She appeared to be looking for a crack in his defense. Reggie hoped his cockeyed smile would fool Fatima but his face revealed he had lied. Fatima began to sniff him like a drug dog. She grabbed his shirt and sniffed it, then reached for his pants zipper.

"What're you doing, Fatima? Ha, ha, Fatima. You buggin' out or sump'n, woman?" Reggie asked, playing her off while struggling against her advances.

She continued, and when satisfied, looked at him. Reggie persisted.

"C'mon, honey stop buggin' and let's get dressed. Let's go.

I promise I'll make it up to you afterwards," he said but Fatima had arrived at her own conclusion.

"What's going on, Reggie?" she asked.

Her eyes penetrated the depths of his soul and in a New York minute, he realized his game was up. Reggie saw the rage building on Fatima's face. Her veins appeared swollen. She stared him up and down before exploding.

"You bastard! You piece a shit!" Fatima shrieked. Then she looked him in the eyes, "You've brought another woman's smell in the sanctity of my temple and violated me, Reggie. Get out now!" Fatima screamed.

Reggie reacted hesitantly as if he needed time to be counted out. Her face was contorted with rage. Fatima started throwing slaps and punches at him. "Get the fuck out! Get your shit and get the fuck out!"

She opened the door and pushed Reggie into the hallway. He stared at her in disbelief.

"Baby, wait. You don't understand. Let me explain," Reggie pleaded.

Fatima slammed the door shut with a loud bang. A second later, she heard knocking on the door.

"Baby, you've gotta believe. There's absolutely nothing going on!"

"You're right," she said, opening the door with tears in her eyes.

Fatima stared at Reggie for a beat. She shook her head and threw his work bag at him. Fatima angrily slammed the door on the befuddled Reggie, scrambled to the sofa, and doubled up on it sobbing.

7:30 p.m.

Claudine walked by Reggie standing in the hallway. She opened the door to her apartment. James was standing by the window looking out. Relief flooded her as he turned to greet her. She finally knew he was alright.

"Honey, you made it home," he said excitedly.

"Yup, I trekked it all the way too," Claudine said, pooped but happy that he was concerned.

"I was worried about you," James said.

"I was thinking about you all day too," she confessed closing her eyes.

"Ditto...I just wanted to make sure you made it home safely. I should probably make my way out of here now. I didn't pack all my stuff, so I'll have to come back later to get it," James said, fumbling for the right words.

Claudine heard him but didn't want to get into another argument. Worse, she didn't want him to leave. Claudine was dying inside.

"I don't know if it's such a wise idea to go out there tonight. I mean, I don't see any reason why you just don't spend the night. Another evening with me isn't going to kill you."

James turned back to looking out the window. He saw candles burning in the distance. It was dark outside. Maybe someone would want to test him, make him a vic. He wanted stay in case someone tried to run up in the apartment.

"I guess you're right," he said shrugging his broad shoulders. They stared at each other and both smiled. "Hey the fridge is still cold so none of the food is spoiled. There's some food waiting on the stove for you," James said.

"Thank you," Claudine said.

"Why don't you rest your feet, I know that walk was murder on your dogs. I'll get you some dinner," James said, walking to the kitchen.

Claudine plopped down on the sofa. She looked up to the ceiling and pumped her fist. "Thank God," she whispered.

**8:00 p.m.**

CJ looked at his watch and finally decided to turn in for the night. By the time he walked into the building, it was so dark, he could barely see his hand in front of his face. Even opening the front door was challenging. Then he remembered the light ornament on his key chain and used it. As CJ entered the darkened hallway, he was momentarily startled by loafers sitting in the stairwell. They nodded at him, clearly meaning no harm. CJ walked into his apartment shutting the door behind him.

Night came with no relief from the heat or humidity. Sol sat across from George, who lounged uncaring, with an unlit cigar dangling from his lips. Sol's ride never showed and they were sharing the humble confines of George's apartment. Still feeling pangs of frustration, Sol glanced around without saying anything. He looked at his watch and all at once, an idea seemed to hit him.

"Whoa! It's eight-thirty," Sol shouted jubilantly looking at his watch. "The Yankees game is on tonight. What channel is ESPN on down here?" he asked George excitedly.

"I don't think it's on anywhere tonight," George deadpanned.

"Damn! What was I thinking? That's why I'm here in the first place."

"So you dig baseball, huh?" George asked with a wry smile.

"Are you kidding me? My father use to take me right down here to Ebbetts Field to watch Dodgers games when I was twelve... and at thirteen I was still going to the games. Yeah, I can say I saw the great Jackie Robinson play." Sol appeared pleased with himself.

"Yes, Jackie Robinson was always cool with me. He was a class act," George said, as if reminiscing.

"That's funny the way you said that. It almost sounded like you knew Jackie Robinson personally. Don't tell me you're one of his...ha, ha, uh cousins?" Sol joked nervously.

"I have an even better one for you." George leaned forward and said, "I played with Jackie."

"Whoa, okay, okay, hold up. Before I jump out of my skin in excitement, you wouldn't happen to be one of those old people who maybe exaggerating just a tad bit about your life to make up for all your shortcomings, would you?"

George removed the unlit cigar momentarily from his lips. He glared at the nervous Sol fidgeting with his collar.

"Sir, you call me a liar again and I will kick your ass out of my apartment into the darkness, you heard me?"

George put the cigar back in his mouth and sat back. Sol thought about the proposition very carefully before he spoke.

"Okay, okay, I'm sorry. I was just checking. Please do tell," Sol said smiling.

"Well, I was always a fine athlete in my youth. During the Second World War, I was stationed in France for two years. After I was discharged, I joined the Negro League and was signed by the Kansas City Monarchs. So in 1946, my rookie year, I played with Jackie, Satchel…a long list of talented players." George smiled nodding. He knew his story had swept Sol away.

"Wow!" Sol exclaimed. He smiled like a kid given the perfect toy by his favorite uncle, and was all ears as George continued.

"That same year, I was traded to the Newark Eagles, and we actually beat the Monarchs for the World Series title. I was twenty-one years old. It was sweet poetic justice. I think I contributed to us winning the title."

"I can't believe I'm talking to a real-life American Negro League World Series champion. So what happened after that? Did you ever see Jackie again?" Sol asked enthusiastically.

"Nope," George said shaking his head. He thought for a beat

then spoke again. "The following year, they signed him to the majors. I was traded to the Brooklyn Giants. After that, the majors started signing up all of our stars, so the league slowly dismantled. I stayed here, where I met my wife, and I've been in Brooklyn ever since," George said with resignation. He leaned back as if deep in thought.

"Damn!" Sol shook his head, dumbfounded.

The sound of guns going off echoed loudly, followed by a sprinkling of sirens coming from emergency vehicles. Sol was clearly terrified by the gunshots and looked to George for some type of comfort. Sol's voice trembled when he spoke.

"I don't suppose by any chance that those were firecrackers, were they?" he joked half-heartedly.

"I'm afraid not," George replied in a matter-of-fact tone.

"I didn't think so," Sol shook his head.

"It's gonna stay this way. You just have to relax," George said nodding toward the streets. Again the sound of gunshots interrupted their conversation.

"Shit, there's a whole lot of shooting going on," Sol said visibly shook. "Hey George, have you ever seen the film, *The Ten Commandments* with Charlton Heston?" Sol asked.

"Of course," George responded with a chuckle.

"Do you remember the scene where Moses tells all the believers to stay in their homes for forty days and nights? And not to open their doors so that evil, diseases and the angel of death will pass their homes, and instead go into the nonbelievers' homes?"

"I remember," George said.

"That's how I feel right now. It's like we're waiting for darkness to pass," Sol said as gunshots echoed. George walked to window and peered outside. He saw that the streets were now pitch black. There were figures lurking everywhere in the darkness. It was impossible to identify anyone until they were close, and then it might be too late. Thugs wearing scowls beneath their bandanas were prowling the streets. The night belonged to them. George pulled the shades down and looked at Sol.

"You want to pray?" George laughed and Sol joined in nervously.

"George, you mind if I ask you a personal question?" Sol asked.

"Go ahead, shoot," George said.

"We're sitting here tonight like two old buddies talking about everything from movies to baseball. This is the most we've ever talked. Well, I guess what I'm wondering is…" Sol's voice trailed as he glanced around the cluttered room. "What happened to you, man?" he asked waving his hand around.

George removed the cigar from the corner of his mouth. He stared at Sol cowering from the sound of gunshots.

"I'll tell you," he said putting the cigar back in a corner of his mouth. "Life happened. You see, there's the life that you plan and there's a life that you're given. I have no regrets. I'm the last person you should ever feel sorry for. I lived a much-fulfilled life. Shit, I've lived five lifetimes."

There was a heavy pause as both men thought about what was said. Sol nodded agreeing.

"You hungry…?" George asked.

"Yeah, I'd have to say I am," Sol answered with a smile.

"I'll fix us something to eat," George said.

"What's on the menu?"

"Frank and beans."

"Frank and beans, huh? Anything else?"

"Yeah," George had the same wry smile. "Beans and franks…"

"Yeah, on second thought, George, I'm gonna call it a night," Sol said loosening his shirt buttons.

"Suit yourself. If you want I can stay out here with you. I'll just sleep right here." George patted the sofa with his hand.

"Hmm, yeah, I think that would be a good idea. I mean you know, for the both of us."

"Right," George said pulling out some pillows and sheets. He threw one of each to Sol before plopping down on the sofa.

"Goodnight, George," Sol said, still studying him.

"Goodnight," George replied. His eyes were closed and a wry smile played across his face.

BlacKout

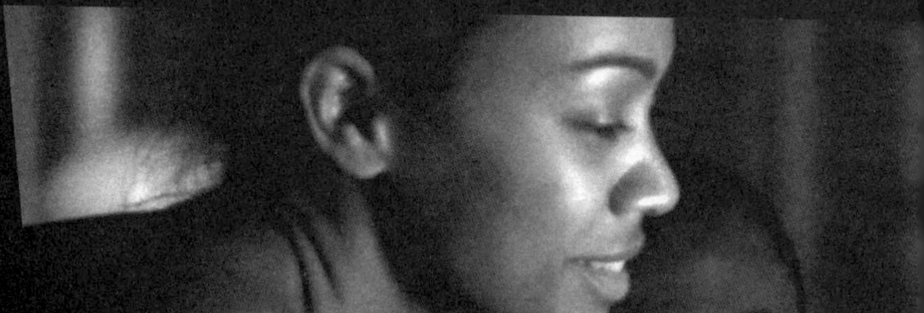

# THIRTEEN

It was around nine-thirty. Despite the heat and madness going on outside, all was cozy inside the apartment of James and Claudine. James put the locks on the door while Claudine lounged with her feet up on the center table. A candle burned close by on the nightstand. Claudine was happy that James hadn't left. The foot rub and dinner she had just received relaxed her to the point of no return. She was ready to reward him for all his efforts.

"Thank you for dinner," she said kissing his hand softly.

"You're welcome, Miss," James said getting close and kissing her lips.

"What happened to your face?" Claudine said when she saw the slight bruise.

"When the power first went off, some of the stores started getting looted. I was on the 'Bush when some cats rushed the electronic store. I ran in there and tried to stop them and got caught up in the scuffle. I'm alright, though."

"Oh my God! Are you sure you're alright?" Claudine asked hugging him close.

"Yes, I'm alright, honey," James nodded. They stayed in each other's embrace without speaking. Then Claudine squeezed James tightly and both laughed quietly.

"We've got a lot to talk about," she said.

"Hmm, hmm," James agreed.

"Let me start, baby," Claudine said.

"The floor is all yours," James responded.

"First, I'm so sorry. Yes, I was starting to get a bit frustrated with our money situation. However, all I could think about today was you. I was so worried about where you might be. I felt so bad because I know I was on your back. Today really put things in perspective about what's important. I don't want to ever take you for granted like that again. I'm sorry."

There was a long pause as James appeared to let the words permeate through him. He swallowed hard before speaking.

"I felt the same way, not being able to reach you and all. First off, I'm glad you're okay. Second, I owe you a huge apology…" James' voice trailed off. He seemed on the verge of breaking down. Claudine moved closer to him.

"Babe, what's wrong?" she asked, gently touching his face.

"I have something important to tell you, boo," James said.

Claudine heard him and her imagination went rummaging through the closet. Oh my God. She hoped and prayed that it wasn't another woman, or the virus. Her heartbeat increased as the tension in the room hit the roof.

"I'm afraid I need help. I'm not well," James said and Claudine held herself trying not to lose it.

"Wha—what's wrong?" she uttered. Claudine was hoping for the best but deep down she feared the worst. All of a sudden things didn't feel as comfortable in the apartment anymore.

"There's a reason why I haven't been able to find work," James said.

"But I know there's a recession…" Claudine began but James raised his hand.

"Let me speak," he said. "I'm experiencing some form of posttraumatic stress disorder. In the beginning, I figured it was natural and that I'd shake it off but it just got worse. It got to the point where I was having difficulty just leaving the apartment. The process I have to go through just to build up courage to step outside these doors. It's crazy, ma."

"James I didn't know. How can I help?" Claudine asked. She was moved to tears, but was happy it wasn't another woman. James continued to speak as she hugged him.

"I spoke with a counselor after you left for work. I'm going to receive help and get myself back on track," James said confidently.

"I'm so sorry, honey," Claudine said, hugging James as tight as she could. "I can't believe I never put it all together. Here I am all this time thinking you don't want to work... I should've known there was something else," she started but James kissed her and they embraced.

"It's alright, baby. It's all good. I made things worst by trying to keep it hidden from you. I realized today that hiding it was only creating a bigger problem."

They hugged in silence. He kissed her gently and they both smiled.

"Don't worry, brown sugar, I'm going to get the man you fell in love with back to you," he said.

"Wasn't that the song we used to sing when we first met?"

"Huh what...?"

"'Brown Sugar'. You said my skin was like brown sugar, then you started singing. 'I want some of your brown sugar'," Claudine hummed the classic R&B tune by D'Angelo.

James joined in singing with her.

*"Brown sugar, babe, I gets high off your love/ I don't know how to behave/I want some of your brown sugar/ I do-ooh..."*

"May I have this dance?" Claudine said as James kept singing.

He smiled when she spoke and took her in his arms. They whirled in happiness to a rhythm that was all theirs. Claudine and

James were in a tight embrace as they danced freely.

"This is alright," James whispered tenderly, his lips against her ear.

"I never lost the man I love. Everything is gonna be all alright, my baby," she said resting her head on his shoulders, cherishing the Moment.

In one smooth motion, James swept her off her feet and carried her into the bedroom. He gently placed her on the bed. She pulled him close and kissed him deep. They rolled around frolicking and laughing like kids do.

"You're my lady," he smiled.

"Oh James, I'm so happy all that stuff is behind us."

Claudine's words were punctuated by an outburst of gunshots. She moved closer to the window and looked outside.

"They're taking advantage of situation," James said coming up behind and closing the shades. "We'll be fine," he said kissing her.

She fell in his arms and he held her, happy to have resolved what had ailed them. He stared in her soft brown eyes. James knew they were on the right road to recovery. Claudine gently kissed his neck and he hugged her so close he could feel her heartbeat intensifying. He hungrily returned her kiss losing all control. He smiled in the darkness, knowing the loss of electrical power had somehow rescued his love.

# FOURTEEN

9:45 p.m.

Hallsboro Project was dark and grim. Two teenage girls walked outside an apartment door and slammed it behind them.

"Don't slam my damn door like that. I don't know why you wanna go over there tonight? It's dark out here," one of the girls said.

"It is, but I want my money before that bitch leaves for Florida."

"How's she gonna do that? Ain't a damn airline leavin' no time soon. You heard it on the radio, didn't you?"

"Oh yeah...? That bitch owes me fifty dollars and I don't want her creepin' outta town with my shit. I want my money."

"There's a blackout, bitch. The whole place is like on lockdown. She ain't goin' nowhere."

"You want your cigarettes and beer, right?" the other asked.

"Ahight, as long as I get my pack o' cigarette and my brew you promise me, I'm cool. C'mon I got that big-ass flashlight ready. Let's roll," one girl said to the next one.

"Damn! This shit b-b-brighten the whole damn place. This a damn good flashlight you brought."

"It's my baby daddy's. He works for transit and knowing his ass, he probably stole the damn thing. Damn no-luck-nigga."

"Ahight, ahight don't start with the same ol' story. Her apartment is only across the next building."

"I know where that bitch apartment at. I lived here all my damn life."

"That ain't my damn problem."

"Well, I need time for my eyes to adjust."

"Let them adjust while we walk. C'mon, you wastin' time. Let's go."

They walked down the long hallway and out of the building using the flashlight to guide them. It was pitch black, and they hurried to their destination.

As soon as they stepped into the darkness, they heard wolf whistles. They girls moved faster and after some distance, they could see dark figures. Under the moonlight and stars the shadowy forms loomed larger.

"Let's go back. Look at all these niggas staring at us like we food or sump'n. It's too creepy out here," the girl who wanted her money back said looking around.

"It's just a few steps away. Keep the flashlight on. Ain't you the one a few minutes ago talking 'bout 'I ain't scared'," the other said.

"Come here, ya bitches!"

"Get 'em bitches over there wid da flashlight!"

The shouts resonated off the building walls and startled the girls. They turned around slowly. Both shuddered when they saw the dark shadows.

"I think they's followin' us. And them niggas look like they up to no good. Let's get the fuck up outta here, Tiny!"

"Her building ain't too far from here. We can make it. Let's run!"

Both girls took off like jets in their Nikes. They headed for the front door of the building as the footsteps got louder behind them.

"Shit! I told you we should've gone at daylight. Them niggas crazy! I don't want none o' them puttin' their hands on me!" One of the girls shouted.

"Rape! Murder! Police!" the girls screamed between their short breaths.

They were running for their lives and reached their former girlfriend's building. Both jumped over construction cones between the road leading to the steps of their destination. They pulled on the door handle.

"Ah shit! It's locked," one of the girls shouted.

"Hurry up, Tiny. Find her bell. Let her buzz us in quick before these niggas catch up," the other girl said, her breath coming in gasps.

"Man, I wanna pee real bad," Tiny said searching for the bell.

"Hurry, you know them crazy-ass might wanna rape us. I can't deal with no shit like that," one said.

"Shine the light on this side, bitch. Ah yeah, I found it. I found it. Shit! It ain't working. Someone is comin' out. Hold the door! Grab the door!"

They busted through the opened door and sprinted to the staircase. The girls flew up three flights of stairs with the goons hot on their trail.

Finding her friend's door, Tiny banged frantically as the footsteps got louder. The goons were closer when a voice came from inside the apartment.

"Who...?"

"It's me, Tiny. Please, please let me in..."

"What d'ya want, Miss Tiny? I ain't got your money...I told you earlier, I'll pay you next week..."

"No please. For real forget about the money."

"What d'ya mean, 'Forget bout the money?'"

"Forget about the money, just let me in, girl, I'll explain later!"

"I don't know about you, after you get up here..."

"Look bitch, some ign'ant Negroes trying to get at us out here. And'em fools look serious. Please let us in. Yes, forget the money, I promise I won't ask you for it as long as I live! Please, please let us in..." she said gasping air.

"Oh, shit! They got guns and I can hear 'em comin' up the stairs!" the other anxiously shouted.

"Give up that flashlight, bitch! I need that!" the goons yelled reaching the floor.

"Oh shit, that nigga gettin' ready to shoot!" the girl screamed frantically.

She threw the flashlight at them and the goons moved out of the way. At the same time, the door was unlocked. The two girls quickly scooted inside just as the goons got nearer. Both let off tremendous sighs of relief once they were inside the apartment.

"Yo Wiz man, fuck 'em bitches, man. They gave up the flashlight," one of the goons said, laughing.

"Yeah, I'd pop some lead in them, but Wiz ain't no fool. I ain't gonna be wastin' no slugs on no bitches. Fuck'em! I just wanna scare they stupid-ass anyway. Shit's fuckin' critical when we chasin' a bitch for her fuckin' flashlight." A smirk slid off the side of his face. He shook his head. "Get the flashlight. Let's go make a real jooks!"

As they walked away, Wisdom returned the gun to his waistband. Laughing, they patrolled the streets in darkness. Tonight there would be no fear in the swagger of these street goons.

"Yo, you saw how them bitches were runnin'?" one of the goons asked, chuckling.

"Yeah, them some real hood rats. They runnin' like they tryin' out for the Olympics," another goon said. They all laughed.

"Fuck 'em, stank bitches! Let's go get some real gold. I got moufs to feed," Wiz said walking away.

# FIFTEEN

**10:20 p.m.**

"Get that vic! Don't let that muthafucka escape!"

Noise echoed in the darkness covering Browser Street. CJ tossed and turned in his crowded bedroom. His small room felt like a sauna, sweat dripped off his back and forehead onto his pillow. CJ awoke to the barking of firearms. He could hear the sound of a police helicopter and saw lights flashing outside his opened window.

Among the shouts, CJ thought he heard the rant of his friends, Khalil and Ty outside. He listened closer and could clearly hear someone sounding like Ty, running off at the mouth. He stuck his head out of the window trying to be sure. It was too dark to identify anyone.

"What y'all doing out there, man?" CJ shouted.

CJ slipped on his shirt and went outside to the street. Fascinated, he stood on the stoop in front of the building, looking up and down. Every few minutes, shadowy figures rushed by him. CJ realized the figures running by didn't even see him. The roar of the police helicopter hovering above drowned out any sounds. He stepped down the stoop and into the street. The helicopter vacated the area and suddenly everything got so quiet, he could have heard a pin drop.

"Ty, you out here, man?" CJ shouted into the darkness.

A dark figure appeared from behind and put CJ in a vicious chokehold. Fear gripped him. He was shocked but tried to fight back. He pulled out his key light out of his pocket and turned it on. CJ peered at his attacker's face.

"So now you see my face, huh? Run your shit, kid."

"Ra, Ra, chill man, chill out! What you doing, man? Yo, you can't be serious," CJ complained while struggling with Rasheed.

"Fuck you! Run all your shit! Think I care you see me?"

CJ slipped out of the chokehold as the two continued tussling. Rasheed pushed CJ against a parked car. Realizing he was in a fight for his life, CJ came back at him with punches. The assailant released a barrage of blows to his face. CJ's adrenaline kicked in and he managed to get off a couple of more punches.

A wave of three goons appeared, seemingly from nowhere and jumped in. They started pummeling CJ. The headlight of an approaching car revealed murderous looks on the street thugs' faces. There was Ty, Khalil and another thug CJ couldn't immediately identify.

"Oh shit! Chill. That's my man CJ," Ty said, jumping back when he recognized the victim.

Rasheed continued kicking CJ furiously down on the asphalt. Khalil and Ty felt guilt-ridden and backed off. Ty stepped up to defend CJ.

"Yo, fuck that. That's my man! Y'all not going to be beating on my man like that," Ty said looking at Rasheed.

"So what you saying…? You and your man gonna take us on? You got knuckle game, nigga?" Rasheed asked with a twisted, evil grin.

"Yo, you know what, fuck you! Fuck that! What's up? Get up, CJ," Ty said knowingly crossing the line.

He had directly challenged Rasheed and was aware of the consequences. Ty couldn't turn his back on helping out a friend in need. He heard Rasheed's mocking tone.

"Wha-a-at!" Rasheed laughed. "Let me find out you got heart. You a ride-or-die-nigga, huh? Yo Khalil, pass the steel."

"Yo Ra, man, c'mon we ain't gotta. We all came up to…" Khalil started to say but Rasheed cut him off.

"Who you wid, nigga? I need to know right now!" Rasheed demanded. Khalil reluctantly gave him the gun. "I'm sorry muthafucka, now what was that you saying?" Rasheed asked waving the gun.

"Nothing," Ty said sheepishly stepping back with his hands

held high.

He knew all the stories about Rasheed being a cold-blooded killer with an itchy trigger finger. Ty didn't want any part of this beef.

"Yeah, I thought so. You's a fake-ass nigga. Watch this, I'm gonna show what kinda fake-ass you are," Rasheed said with a chuckle. He walked up to Ty and shoved the gun in his hand. "What nigga! Go ahead bust me!" Rasheed said watching Ty fumbling with the gun in his hand.

"I ain't trying to do that. Yo, you m-my m-man," Ty said, his voice trembling.

Rasheed took the gun away and returned the clip inside of it. His laugh was mocking.

"I know you ain't crazy. But I only gave you half a chance anyway. You official, right? You wanna be down, right? Peel this nigga's wig back right here and now," Rasheed ordered.

"I...I don't know if that's right..."

"You say he's a show-off, right? Then let me see you blast him. You know what? You don't have a choice. Shoot this bird-ass nigga!"

Ty was trembling so hard you could hear his teeth chatter. Terrified, he slowly pointed the gun at CJ.

"Yo, that's my word. If you don't smoke this nigga, I'm not gonna kill y'all...just yet. You know what I'm gonna do? I'm gonna take you two down to the basement, and straight torture you muthafuckas. Then after that, I'll kill you and dude. I'm gonna kill y'all ugly-ass moms too just for fun."

CJ saw Ty raising the gun and taking aim at his dome. He couldn't figure out what was happening and pleaded with his friend.

"Ty, what you doing man? Don't do this. This was what I was talking about..."

"Lemme see, your ugly-ass moms is in apartment 4C, right? And your stupid-ass moms, she still in 1D, cool. I'm going to pay those bitches a visit later tonight," Rasheed said.

CJ looked in Ty's face and realized that Rasheed was getting to him. Ty had a sick grin on his face and CJ hated to think that this could be his end. Tears rolled down his face. He held his breath and braced himself for the inevitable.

"I'm waiting, nigga. I don't have all night. What's it going to be? I done called you out! I got witnesses. After tonight it's a wrap for you, baby-boy," Rasheed spat his words of wrath and knew it was affecting Ty.

A look of torment covered Ty's face. His hand holding the gun shook. Ty was caught in the vice grip of a deadly catch-22. All the while CJ kept trying to reach him.

"Don't listen to him Ty. Follow your own mind," CJ said. "Yo Ty, I love you like a brother, that's all I got to say."

"I'm gonna count to three and then you better push this nigga's wig back," Rasheed announced. "What's it gonna be, bitch?" Rasheed's voice thundered.

Ty looked at CJ's bloodied face. His left eye was completely swollen shut. They were always childhood friends. There was pity in Ty's eyes. CJ didn't beg for his life. He was doubled over moaning in agony. Ty stood a couple of feet away, nervously pointing the loaded gun.

"One…! You think I'm fucking playing with you?"

A car drove by the corner and as it passed them, the silhouettes of the group and CJ leaning up against a car were briefly illuminated by the headlights.

"Two…!" Rasheed counted.

**11:00 p.m.**

There was a sudden spark in the midst of the darkness. A single gunshot rang out and echoed for what seemed an eternity. Ty looked at the smoking gun still in his hand. His eyes popped wide open and he sweated profusely. He bent his head down and sobbed like a baby. CJ was shocked. He looked down at his shirt turning crimson from his blood. Khalil was completely stunned. He slowly backed up a few paces. Rasheed grabbed the gun from Ty.

"Now that's gangsta! You family now, son. I got you. Go ahead man, run. I'll clean this mess up so no one will know you were here."

Rasheed looked at the gun as Ty took off running. He glanced down at CJ in the throes of dying.

"You's a dumb muthafucka. That's why I've never liked your ass! All you had to do was run your shit, bitch-ass. All of a sudden you wanna act hard!"

Rasheed savored the moment for a few seconds, watching as CJ's body leaked blood. He heard CJ's gurgle as the injured teen gasped for air.

"Guess now you won't be walking around the block like you better than everyone else, huh? You ain't shit!"

Rasheed spat on CJ then he fired another round in his torso and walked away. CJ's breathing was labored. His body twitched in pain.

At that very moment, Ms. Thompson's eyes opened from her deep sleep. She awoke frantic. Something didn't feel right. Ms. Thompson searched through the apartment with a candle looking for her only child.

"CJ, CJ, where are you?"

She opened the door of his bedroom, only to find an empty bed. A streak of panic ran through her entire body. Swallowing hard, Ms. Thompson used one hand to hug herself. The other carried a lit candle. She looked around like she was lost in her own home. Opening the window she called out his name. Outside was dark and she saw the figures but was unable to identify anyone.

"CJ, CJ," she whispered, becoming even more anxious.

She was desperate to find her son and slowly made her way to the door. Ms. Thompson reluctantly unlocked her door and carefully opened it. She called out her son's name in a short, firm whisper.

"CJ..."

It was dark in the hallway and out of nowhere a figure lunged at Ms. Thompson. She was startled by a man who tried to push his way in. Ms. Thompson screamed and attempted to lock the door but the man's hand was preventing her from closing the door.

"Ma'am, I just need some water, please! I'm not going to hurt you, Miss. I just want some water!" the voice reasoned.

"No! Get away!" Ms. Thompson shrieked.

The person kept pushing against the door as Ms. Thompson screamed hysterically trying to close it. Finally she was able to lock the door and broke down crying on the floor. After a minute she got up and found the phone, hoping for a miracle. It was dead. Frustrated and still crying, she threw it against the wall. Ms. Thompson sat on the floor and cried without really knowing why.

# SIXTEEN

Friday, August 15, 2003, 12:30 a.m.

Rasheed and his goons successfully broke into the sneaker store. Before rushing inside, he pulled out the gun and handed it to Ty.

"Take this man. You've earned the right to carry the weight. Handle the steel with care," Rasheed said with a smirk.

He was now officially down with the gang but Ty appeared every bit terrified and hesitated as the gun was passed to him.

"I don't wanna," Ty started. He saw the screw tighten on Rasheed's face. Ty fell back into place. "Ahight man, I got it this time."

"Yarned it, nigga. Now you in," Rasheed grinned.

Rasheed kept the group in check using intimidation to rule. Ty vomited before entering the store. He badly wanted to walk away but the gun was on him. He tried to control his fast beating heart. He thought about smoking weed and chilling with L. Ty had walked across the point of no return in his worst nightmare.

They entered the store and Ty fearfully scrambled through boxes of sneakers. Armed with flashlights, they grabbed sports apparel by the box-loads.

"Yo, we racking up tonight, for real," Rasheed said exultantly.

"Let's not get too greedy. Right now what we have is good. Let's bounce," Khalil said.

"Man, fuck that! You stupid? How many chances like this you think we gonna have again? Ain't no alarms going off tonight, dogs! Tonight, the streets of New York is deaf, blind and mute," Rasheed proclaimed. "And she's getting fucked. Big time!" He ran around looking at all the merchandise and ordered. "Yo, you two go upstairs and start bringing boxes down here!"

**12:45 a.m.**

Two goons ran upstairs with flashlights ready. They heard the police sirens and froze. Two police were coming inside and others were racing toward the store ready to bag all the goons downstairs.

"Don't make us chase you! Freeze…!"

"Damn! I don't wanna go to prison," Ty said.

Ty saw Rasheed take off running and quickly followed behind

him. They ran to the window, opened it, and jumped onto the fire escape leading to the top of the building. Although it was dark, the moonlight offered enough light for them to navigate. Ty was breathing hard and running fast to keep up with Rasheed. They were sprinting across the rooftop.

A couple of moments later, they reached the edge of the building and searched for the fire escape. There was none.

"Damn! What da fuck! We gotta jump across the fucking building," Rasheed hissed through his heavy breathing.

"What da fuck you say we gon' do?" Ty asked looking around frantically. "Po-po is on us, Ra."

"Yeah, I see'em muthafuckas coming. Let's hide, but you may have to use that gat, fam."

Four police descended on them in pairs. A roaring helicopter hovering overhead shined a bright spotlight on them. Ty and Rasheed scampered around in search of a place to hide but they were out of luck. The officers closed in on them with guns and flashlights drawn.

"Show me your fucking hands!" one of the officers shouted to the pair

"Drop all your weapons!" another ordered.

"Get on the ground!" another ordered.

Their shouting mixed with the sound of the buzzing helicopter discombobulated Ty for a beat. He reached into his pocket and pulled out the gun. It was a deadly mistake. The police simultaneously squeezed their triggers. Rasheed and Ty were caught in a hail of bullets. Round after round crashed into Ty's body from every angle, lifting him off the roof. He fell dead onto the streets below.

"Oh shit!" Rasheed yelled when the bullets tore into his leg. He fell squirming holding his leg.

"I been shot, I been shot…"

They moved in quickly and handcuffed the bleeding Rasheed. The officers shone their flashlights and saw Ty laid out on the street below.

"Fucking more paper trail," one of the officers said.

Meanwhile, back inside the store, the police were trying to round up the other goons.

"Come out, come out now! And keep your hands up! Everyone come out where we can see you. This is my last fucking warning!" he announced. Slowly, each young man emerged from his hiding place. The police went through searching each gang member.

"Do you have any fucking weapons on you?" an officer asked, pointing his gun.

"Please don't shoot me. Don't shoot me, please. I don't have any weapons on me sir," Khalil said holding both hands high and walking forward to the police.

The cops ransacked the store and led each gang member out

in handcuffs. Two cops roughed up another goon and slammed him to the ground.

"I'm gonna have to add resisting arrest to the list of charges," one officer said.

"Spread your muthafucking legs," another police shouted at Khalil.

"Alright, let's take these assholes in," a cop said.

As he was led outside Khalil's face registered shock when he saw Rasheed being carted off cuffed into an ambulance. A body bag containing Ty was being zipped.

"I think this is it, we've got the other two who were on the roof," one of the officers said to his partner.

Khalil grimaced. It seemed like a nightmare that he wished he could wake up from.

1:30 a.m.

A trail of blood outlined the fate of CJ. He managed to drag himself near the front steps of his building. His jersey was soaked in his own blood. Every painful step was a major journey as he attempted to make his way into the building. CJ encouraged himself forward, motivating his bloodied body up each step.

"No way! I can't go out like this," he whispered as he felt himself losing his grasp on his life. CJ panicked and started crying again. "No, not like this. Not like this. Not like this, God, please," he pleaded dragging himself up the steps.

He stopped at the middle step. With the last spurt of energy he could muster, CJ tried to get up onto the next step but collapsed.

**1:50 a.m.**

The two goons Rasheed sent upstairs at the sneaker store finally emerged. They crept around the ransacked store perplexed as to what to do next. They tiptoed through the stacks of boxes littering the store. As they were about to leave, one of them pulled out a lighter and lit a T-shirt hanging on a rack. They took off as the shirt went up in flames.

**1:55 a.m.**

Inside the bedroom of their apartment, Claudine and James lay in bed sweating. She was wrapped in his arms, her head resting softly on his muscular chest. Claudine opened her eyes, went to the window, and peered out into the creepy, quiet darkness. It was as if evil had passed through the neighborhood. Claudine smelt a strong odor of something burning coming from the outside.

"James, James," she cried out anxiously. "Wake up."

"Baby, what is it?" James responded groggily.

"Don't you smell that?" she asked shaking James.

"Huh, what…?"

"I think there's fire on the other side of the building."

"Baby, please come to bed. We've been up all night. There's nothing we can do about it. Just come to bed."

"I know there's something burning pretty bad out there," Claudine said with concern.

"Go to sleep, babe," James said still half asleep.

Claudine was apprehensive and continued looking out the window. There was nothing to see but her curiosity wouldn't allow her to leave the window. She whispered a quiet prayer of hope.

"God bless us all. Please get us through the night."

She eased back down in the bed next to James and closed her eyes but was having difficulty getting back to sleep. Claudine stared at the ceiling until she eventually fell into her own world of darkness.

# SEVENTEEN

Friday, August 15, 2003, 5:00 a.m.

The sun rose on the lifeless, bloody body of CJ lying on the steps of the building. The early morning sounds of birds chirping were heard. Police radio squawked as an officer moved toward the body and checked for a pulse. He immediately got back on his radio and called for back up.

It was 5:25 a.m. when policemen, patrol cars and an ambulance descended on the tragic scene in front of the building. The police questioned those standing around while paramedics examined the body.

5:45 a.m.

Inside her apartment, Ms. Thompson was curled up on the floor. Having stayed up all night worrying about her son, she was a complete wreck. Ms. Thompson was sure that something terrible had happened to CJ, but still she was startled by a forceful knock on the door.

Ms. Thompson's throat tightened up and her lips went dry. There was more knocking, louder this time.

"Is anyone home? Open up. This is the police!"

The loud knocks on the door rang in Ms. Thompson's head. She developed an instantaneous and intense headache. She wanted to pretend that there was no commotion outside her door. Ms. Thompson sensed that once the door was opened she was going to have to deal with her son's fate.

"No!" Ms. Thompson yelled pulling on her hair. "Please go away, please. Don't tell me something happened to my baby, no!"

"Miss, open the door, please!" The police shouted, knocking even louder.

**6:00 a.m.**

A crowd assembled outside 254 Browser Street. People were in disbelief. Kids squeezed past the adults and officers and peeked. A white sheet was placed over CJ's body. Fatima wept. Even the West Indian women were in shock and became emotional.

"Jesus, mi can't believe they killed that poor woman's child," Beatrice said, rocking back and forth.

"I don't wish nothing like this on no mother. Just yesterday this woman was out praising her child and for him to be found dead, murdered like this. It's going to kill her." Sister Carol cried as she spoke.

"Okay," Fatima said raising her hands to get the attention of everyone. "Everyone needs to go in their buildings and check with their neighbors to make sure that everyone is alright, please! Check your family and neighbors and make sure everyone is okay."

Fatima signaled for two young men to accompany her inside the building. Fatima knocked on the first door she came to and waited. She did successive doors until she came to the third floor and knocked on Ms. Germaine's door. It swung opened and Fatima cautiously walked inside.

"Ms Germaine, Ms. Germaine, you inside...?"

Fatima continued down a short corridor that opened into the living room. She checked each room. "Ms. Germaine, are you in here?" she asked looking inside the woman's bedroom.

"Oh my God! Ms. Germaine!" Fatima exclaimed when she spotted Ms. Germaine on the floor on her stomach.

The news had spread like wildfire all over East Flatbush. CJ was a positive teen who was not into violence. He had strived to learn and was on his way out of the hood to study. Getting shot and dying in front of his building was not the way anyone envisioned him going out. Those who knew him were filled with fury and restless.

Around 7:30 a.m., Claudine and James came outside the building to find the crowd. They saw the yellow tape around the side steps of the building. There were detectives everywhere gathering evidence. CJ's mother was sobbing hysterically as uniformed officers attempted to console her. A group of teenage girls sat on the steps crying.

"Oh shit!" James shouted immediately.

"What's going on? What happened?" Claudine asked.

"They shot CJ last night. They found him right here on the steps this morning. Yeah, that's what it do," Corey said.

"Oh God! Is he alright?" Claudine asked visibly shaken.

"Nah, he died," Corey said shaking his head.

"No! No! Don't say that!" Claudine wailed.

James embraced her, holding her close to him. Her breathing became shallow and Claudine beat her fist against James' chest. Finally she broke down crying. James continued holding her as Claudine's breath came in gasps. She looked as if she was about to collapse.

"Why would someone want to kill CJ? For what? Why James? Can you tell me?" Claudine wailed.

"I don't know, baby. I don't know," James said, hugging Claudine.

Even the some of the young men couldn't refrain from crying and loudly cursing in rage. The police kept a heavy presence at the scene and tried to keep the incensed crowd under control.

It was 8:00 in the morning and the sun was in full splendor. Rumbling was heard as clean-up crews worked to repair damages to stores. Nelson, Rick, Cam, Tech and L from the barbershop walked over from the other end of the block. They stood behind Claudine and James.

"You heard what happened?" Nelson asked grimly.

"Yeah man, I can't believe that shit," James said in disgust.

"These young kids out here be wilding these days. You feel me? I bet you a young idiot did that. They the grimy ones," Nelson said balling up his fist.

"Son didn't deserve to go out like that though. CJ was doing his thing, going to school hard body," L said shaking his head. "That's fucked up. Somebody outside of the neighborhood did that shit, you know that, right?"

"Baby, I bumped into him just yesterday when I was coming home from work yesterday. I was telling him not to stay outside too late. And look at what happened," Claudine said.

"I'm sayin', lights go out for one night and muthafuckas don't know how to act," Rick said.

"You been out on the 'Bush yet?" L asked.

"No, what happened?" James asked.

"Ah man, mad fires. Mad, fucking lootin'. They burned down Sneaker World," Tech said, exasperation in his voice.

"Are you serious?" James asked in surprise.

"That's my word, one hun'red," Tech said in finality. "I'm a go see my man up in C6 for a minute." Tech ran up the stairs and disappeared inside the building.

"Man, I've been going to that spot since I was in junior high," James said.

"That was where CJ worked," Cam added.

"I bought my first pair of Jordans at Sneaker World," L said in shock.

Some of the teenage girls began to assemble flowers, candles and cards on the spot where CJ was murdered. They somberly constructed a makeshift shrine to the fallen teen.

Claudine watched for a minute then became overwhelmed by the emotion. She took off crying.

"Baby, wait!" James said following quickly behind her.

"This makes no kind of sense," Claudine cried.

Suddenly she stopped in her tracks and James caught up to her. They saw the fire trucks and firefighters who spent most of the night putting out fires. There were at least two burnt-out stores.

"Oh God, why…?" Claudine asked in wide-eyed surprise.

**9:00 a.m.**

People came out of their homes to witness the postwar-like atmosphere. Most of the stores were closed with their gates down. Traffic lights were not functioning and police officers were on the streets directing traffic. A handful of vendors were trying to sell the remaining food they had left without letting customers inside the stores. The Korean family stood outside Sneaker World, assessing damages. James and Claudine walked further down the avenue, stepping over shards of broken glass everywhere. Devastated by the sight, she leaned heavily on James' shoulder as they walked back home. Fatima was out front rousing an already fired-up crowd.

"What the fuck are you guys doing? Why, please tell me why? You're killing your own. CJ was gonna make something of his life! He represented you and he represented you," she pointed at concerned neighbors. "He was one of our finest products and you shattered everything!" Fatima shouted hysterically.

Some of the young kids stared at Fatima as if she was a lunatic. Others were too numb to understand her. There were those who played stupid and refused to take responsibility for anything. With all the angry shouting and screaming going on, James felt that something might erupt. He pulled Claudine closer to the building.

By 10:00 a.m., police officers started arriving en masse and ordered the crowd to disperse. This only infuriated the crowd and tensions boiled over.

"When we gwine get power back on?" Sister Carol asked.

The police officer ignored the woman and rushed over to Fatima. When the officer touched her, Fatima went off like a firecracker.

"First of all don't touch me! Don't touch me, alright? This is a free country. I'm on my block! If I wanna speak my mind, I can do that!" Fatima shouted.

"What it do! That's some bullshit!" Corey shouted.

The officer walked over to Corey and got in his face. "You got a problem, chief?" he asked with his hand on his gun while staring Corey down.

"Hell yeah, I got a problem!" Corey shouted in the officer's face. "They killed my man out here today. What it do? Y'all ain't doing shit about it!"

"You need to lower your voice," the officer said.

"Where the hell was you? Any other time, y'all be on every corner breathing down our necks. What it do, huh?" Corey shouted.

"Somebody need to get Al Sharpton!" an onlooker shouted.

"Who got Brother Sharpton's number?" someone else asked.

**10:30 a.m.**

The crowd became more agitated. Its curses and abusive rhetoric toward the police was getting out of hand. James held onto Claudine and pulled her into the building. Claudine went into a rampage as she entered the apartment.

"James, they killed CJ. I just can't believe they killed him. For what? What reason would someone have for killing him?" Claudine asked, her frustration escalating.

"I can't give you the answer, baby."

"What the hell is happening?" she asked. "I never thought it would get this crazy! We're hurting our own neighborhood. It wasn't like this in the city. You should've seen it, people were helping one another."

"This is Brooklyn. It ain't the city," James said.

"James, we have to go back out there and set these people straight," Claudine said heading to the door.

"No, we're not going anywhere. We have enough water and hopefully enough food to last us through the night," James said holding her.

"Why shouldn't we help?"

"Hitting the streets isn't going to do us any good but get us hot and more pissed off, Claudine. Look, why don't you go lay down and take a nap. I'm sure by the time you wake up, the power will be back on and everything will be alright."

"And what if it isn't, James? Then what, huh? What are we gonna do? What are we going to eat if we go another night without power? I'm about to lose my mind. This doesn't make any sense to me!"

Claudine stomped away and James attempted to stop her. She was irritated and he was unsure what was really on her mind.

"Baby, where are you going?" James asked.

"I'm gonna lay down," she said walking to the bedroom.

She crawled into the bed and curled up in the fetal position. Claudine cried herself to sleep.

A few minutes later, James went to the kitchen and sat down trying not to think too hard. He was feeling better that Claudine was able to sleep. James walked to the bathroom and stared at himself in the mirror. He was hot and sweaty. He splashed water on his face, hair and his chest. His mind slowly drifted to the events of 9/11, and he remembered the panic and mayhem.

*Firefighters were running into the building and police officers were giving orders to pedestrians. They were working nonstop trying everything possible to save people's lives.*

The blackout jarred his memory. He realized he was doing everything possible to hold on to his sanity. Without drying himself, James lay on the couch and took heed of his own advice. He decided to sleep the day away. It was 11:00 a.m.

# EIGHTEEN

The block was crowded with people. Frustration filled the air and made it very tense. The crowd remained restless as people were outraged at CJ's death. The rising temperature and humidity did nothing to help ease the situation. Food and water were scarce and people were looking for answers.

Around 11:15 a.m. two paramedics came out of the building carrying Ms. Germaine on a stretcher. Some of the older folks rushed to see what was wrong with her. Many were just curious while others genuinely cared.

"Are you okay, Ms. Germaine?" Fatima asked. "How are you feeling?"

"I'll be fine, dear. I'll be alright…" Ms Germaine said as she was being wheeled away.

"Ms. Germaine, Ms. Germaine, how yuh doing…?" Beatrice asked.

"Oh don't worry 'bout me. God will help me," Ms. Germaine answered.

"I'm gwine with her to the hospital," Beatrice said walking with the paramedics.

"Are you a family member?" the paramedic asked.

"Mi like family, mi is her best friend for twenty years now…"

"You've got to be a family member to ride with her. We're taking her to Brooklyn Hospital," the paramedic said.

"It's about time you got here. I called about a hour ago. She could've died. What, you guys forgot about us down here in the hood?" Fatima shouted at the paramedics.

They ignored her ranting, and put Ms. Germaine into the ambulance. Tech walked out of the building and saw the EMS leaving with Ms. Germaine. He carried a big bag of goods in his arm.

"Yo, what happened to Ms. Germaine?" Tech paused to ask Fatima.

"She went through the whole evening yesterday without any food or insulin for her diabetes, and she passed out," Fatima said.

"That's messed up one hun'red. She gonna be alright?" Tech asked.

"She's gonna be fine, my brother, just fine. They can't keep us down, Black man! Nothing is new under the sun. They've tried this before. It keeps coming back three-sixty. Now it's our generation's turn to sustain!" Fatima said, becoming more intense.

Tech didn't want to hear the lecture and picked up his bag. He decided to keep moving but Fatima was in no mood for passive behavior.

"Tech wait, hold up, take this," Fatima said, handing him a flyer.

Tech took the paper and examined the handwritten flyer with a cynical smirk on his grill. He shook his head as an officer watched him and Fatima closely.

"I'm trying to get the word out in the community and round everyone up so we can file a claim against the city. As a matter of fact, here, take some I have enough..." Fatima continued.

"Nah, nah I ain't the one, yo. One hun'red, I'm not political," Tech said walking away quickly. He could hear Fatima still preaching behind him.

"We gotta rise up and take control of our lives...Wait up, the people have to know. Folks need to take pictures of all the food that went bad last night. The city is liable, yo!" Fatima shouted.

When Tech did not respond the way she wanted him to, Fatima turned to the West Indian women on the stoop.

"Here you go, ladies. I need you to go home and take pictures of all the food you had to throw out yesterday. I'm going to show you how to get paid!" Fatima said handing out flyers.

Both West Indian women read the flyer. They looked nonchalantly at Fatima. Beatrice spoke finally.

"Cha-man! Why ya talk bout, heh? Tek pictures of what? The

city ain't gonna do a damn thing. She better move from mi! That lickle girl is mad. Mad, you know?"

"Hmm, hmm, you got that right," Sister Carol said nodding in agreement. They went back to looking for more drama on the street.

11:30 a.m.

Tech walked down to the barbershop where the crew was lounging out front. He put the bag inside the barbershop. They had front row seats to all the madness and were busy discussing the recent events.

"Yo, what I missed?" Tech asked as he walked up to where the rest stood.

"Nothing that you wanna see now," Rick deadpanned. "I'm sayin' I still can't believe they murked son like that. We were just kicking it with him yesterday," he continued.

"Everyone on the block had mad love for CJ. I'm telling you, it had to be one of them muthafuckas from the projects. You know the projects be breeding 'em raunchy muthafuckas. That's my word, I better not see anyone from Hallsboro walk through this block today," L said putting his hands up. "It ain't gonna be nice."

"Word, that's what's up..." Cam joined in.

"What's up with you, L?" Tech asked sensing the rage burning in L.

"I ain't eat since yesterday, yo. I'm surprise my lips ain't chalked up hard body like Pookie in New Jack City. I can't even use my fucking ATM card," L complained.

"Here man, go to the store. You know Ali will let you hold sump'n until you get paid," Nelson said.

"Ah c'mon, Nel, Ali is in this the same as us. Where he gonna find fresh food from? Out his ass...?" L asked.

"I heard all them cats got bunked up last night. Lil, Smooth, Sin, all of them," Cam said.

"Good! They the ones keeping the block down. Ty and Lil had no business rolling with those other dudes. Now they gonna have to find out that prison ain't nothing to brag about, you feel me?" Nelson said.

"That's one hun'red," Tech agreed.

"They fucked up," Nelson said quickly. "The system now is different. Back in the day, if you got caught up, you did the time and put that shit behind you. If you were lucky, you'd take your stash, flip it then start a little business. Ain't no winners in that game now," Nelson said.

"Shit, last night was even deadlier than you think," Tech said. "My man in C6 told me that Ty was pushed off the roof of the sneaker store and cops shot Rasheed."

"Get da fuck outta here," Cam said.

"Say what?" Nelson asked.

"Wha I told y'all? I'm sayin' that nigga was just bad news," Rick said. "No wonder it was sounding like Iraq out here last night, dog," Rick added with a chuckle.

"Fucking Ty! Damn! You hate to see a young nigga go out like that. He could've done sump'n with his life instead of running with a knucklehead like fucking Rasheed," Nelson said.

"My man said Rasheed in the hospital, under arrest. And that's one hun'red," Tech said.

"Good for his ass. Yo Tech, man, I'm sayin' you should've talked to Ty," Rick said.

"I tried. He wanted to be a gangsta, get a rep. And plus he mostly talked to L," Tech said. "They was always burnin' trees."

"That nigga wasn't trying to hear no one, dogs. We'd smoke and I'd kick it to dude. It be in one ear and out the other. Ty wanted to run with Rasheed and have everyone fearing him. He be flippin'," L said shaking his head.

"We lost two young brothers in less than a day, and we probably gonna lose some more before this shit's all over with. But we gotta start doing better with these young'uns. It's up to us to let them know when they shit ain't right, you feel me?" Nelson said.

"Them young kids, they ain't tryin' a hear us, Nel. We old school and they new school, they gonna do what they wanna. Ty and Lil don't wanna hear shit from heads like us," Tech said.

"Yeah, then we gotta find a way to reach these youths, man. We gotta start working to better our families, physically, spiritually and mentally. And we gotta do that for our community. It's up to us grown-ups to make a difference."

"I hear that one hun'red!"

"That's what's up for real!"

"We gotta go hard body!"

"Yeah, but kids nowadays into themselves. Videogames got their minds on lock and they ain't trying to see your point of view, Nel. They want the nice whips and quick dough that's why they run behind niggas like Rasheed and ignore what you trying to kick," Rick said.

"These kids gotta be reached because they're our future, you feel me?" Nel said.

"Word, they are, but all they wanna do is bang and slang, hard body. Shit's crazier now. That's my word!" L said shaking his head. "Girls don't wanna eat at Mickey D's no more. You gotta buy 'em filet mignon. Shit done changed a lot."

"We gotta teach them. If each one teaches one, pretty soon the whole community will get the lesson," Nelson said.

"Television shows be teaching them. Even the videogames

are too violent. And bust this, my daughter wanna play *Grand Theft Auto*," Rick laughed.

"They destroying the minds of our children with these air-head programs 'bout nothing," Tech said.

"Yeah, but you producing music make some positive shit. Let L make a song rapping about some positive shit. You feeling me on that?" Nelson asked giving Tech a pound.

"Yeah, but what if that don't sell. I gotta make music that's gonna keep my career going, hard body," L opined.

"I'm telling you, last night, them cats were straight bum-rushing into peoples' apartments on some larceny shit. They were out looking for theirs the ski-mask way, they'll catch a bad one every now and then. That's what's up," Cam said pointing her finger for emphasis.

"I wish a nigga would try some shit and ransack my home. Shit, I purposely stayed in front of my door, leaned back on my chair with the Glock cocked, resting on my lap. Just waiting, hard body," L said.

"That's one hun'red, you sound like you were ready," Tech laughed.

"Word up," L continued. "I wouldn't even say anything if I saw them breaking in. As they start walking in, they'd have just seen sparks go off in the darkness. Blacka! Blacka! Blam! Blam!"

Everyone laughed.

"Fuck that. I'm sayin', I'm not a fighter. I leave all that shit alone and linked up with my shortie from Lincoln Place. And I spent the blackout bangin' her back out. Fucked around and damn near caught a heat stroke," Rick said chuckling. "You know me... I'll be doing my thing till the early morn."

About 11:45 a.m., Toothless Tone came strolling pass the barbershop. He stopped and stared at the crew sitting out front.

"Ha, ha, ha, what I told y'all yesterday? I told y'all they trying to kill us. They ain't gonna turn shit back on, until every last one of y'all has dropped dead like cockroaches. I told you. Hey, give me a dollar, young blood."

"Man, you better get out of here. That's what's up," Cam said giving the derelict the brush-off. All the others agreed and shooed Tone away. "It's too hot for that shit, Tone," Cam continued.

Toothless Tone stared at her for a beat before he spoke. "You think it's too hot, huh? Well it's gonna get hotter, you damn freak!"

The guys all laughed as Toothless Tone continued to speak.

"I just heard it on the radio, the power has been restored in Shea Stadium and the Mets game against Colorado Rockies won't be cancelled tonight."

"What...?" Nelson asked, his eyebrows knitted in genuine concern.

"That's right. They can light up that big-ass stadium. All 'em fuckin' millionaires running around in their tights, swinging bats at a lil' white ball. But they won't light up the ghetto for you guys so you can eat, wash your ass or use your phones," Toothless Tone said mockingly.

"Huh uh," Cam said shaking her head in dismay.

"Yessir!" Toothless Tone continued. "You best believe they gonna make that baseball paper. The mayor's gonna be in Flushing tonight watching the Rockies get their asses kicked. America's favorite pastime, baby!" Toothless Tone nodded and continued with his stroll feeling victorious.

"Ain't that about a bitch? How they gonna light up that big-ass stadium and then talk bout there ain't no power? It's politics as usual. That's some bullshit," L said.

"You right, it might be politics. There's no real money to be made in the hood. So why rush to bring power here? Then again, this could be some kind of corporate diversion. I don't put it past the peeps at Enron," Nelson said.

"Enron, Eron...that name sounds familiar. Don't that dude live down the block?" Cam quizzed.

Everyone turned and looked at her like she was crazy. Cam still didn't get it and continued in her ignorance.

"What? I'm saying, there's a dude down the block name Enron!"

"Yo, chill with that, Cam. You're embarrassing me right now, one hun'red," Tech said walking a little way off.

An old man walking by with a transistor radio playing loud interrupted the gathering as they listened to the news broadcast.

*"Temperature will reach in the upper nineties today and in the news at the 12 o'clock hour, Con Ed is reporting that power has been restored to Times Square and Broadway. This is your twenty-four news station..."*

A chorus of boos rained down and the old man moved on with his radio.

"Ah man, that's not right…" Tech said.

"See, I told y'all," L said.

"C'mon man, let's take a walk around the block and find out what's going on," Nelson suggested to the rest of the group.

Tech, L, Rick and Cam nodded in agreement.  They got up and started down the block toward the bodega.

# NINETEEN

**12:30 p.m.**

Browser Street, Brooklyn, was still humid and fry-an-egg-on-the-sidewalk hot, but people were revved up. Many questions remained unanswered for the people crowding the pavements. A long line of customers waited to buy water and unspoiled food outside Ali's bodega. The barbershop crew walked while exchanging friendly disses. Ali, like all the other vendors who remained opened, sold through a small opening in his door. Customers were not allowed to enter the store. Beatrice was at the front of the line talking to Ali.

"Ali, yesterday you gave me the wrong juice and chips, mon. Let me come inside and pick out what I want, mon. I can't shop like this," Beatrice said.

"Sorry, sweetheart, I can't do that. For now, we have to keep it regulated. Next! Who's next?" Ali said.

"Ali, you have anymore candles?" Keisha asked with tear-stained face. She had already used some on the makeshift shrine for

"I' sorry we ran out of candles.  Who's next?"

An army jeep with National Guard troops sped by.

A street vendor walked along the line selling batteries from his knapsack. "Batteries, batteries! Don't get caught with no batteries. Don't be left in the dark.  I got double A's right here.  Keep your radios on!" he shouted.

"I'm sayin' this shit's crazy!" Rick said as the barbershop crew continued down the block, stunned by the looting.

"I'm telling you man, one hun'red we living in the last days," Tech said.

"It's survival of the fittest, that's what's up, dog," Cam chimed in.

"At the rate we're going in this country, we keep messing with everybody else, this is how everyday life's gonna be," Nelson declared.

"Let's get some water.  I'm hotter than a mother," L said.

A crowd of people surrounded a Rastafarian man selling bottled water from a cooler filled with blocks of ice.  The crew walked over, Nelson addressed the street vendor.

"Dread man, the water's cold, right?"

"Very cold, my brother," the vendor replied.

"Alright, let me get five of those.  How much?" Nelson asked.

"Ten dollars, my brother," the vendor said.

"What? That shit's a dollar at the store," Cam said.

The vendor took the bottle from Cam's hand and continued selling other customers. The barbershop crew was pissed as they walked away.

"Everybody's trying to get over now, that's what's up," Cam said.

"It's about to get gully out here, I'm sayin'," Rick said.

"For real, now I'm starting to get vex. They better turn this muthafucka on so I can have access to my money hard body. I'm hungry, yo! This shit ain't funny no more," L complained.

"It never was," Nelson added.

**2:15 p.m.**

Claudine and James had heard a lot of questions about the blackout and not enough answers. Devastated by CJ's death, they retired to the safety of their bedroom, and Claudine fitfully slept. James watched her for a while, and then walked into the kitchen in search of peace and something to eat.

WELCOME
TO
BROOKLYN

**2:30 p.m.**

Claudine was in her bedroom and slowly opened her eyes. She automatically glanced at the alarm clock. It was blank and she sighed in disappointment. She got out of the bed and went to the kitchen where James was eating cereal.

"Any updates?" she asked opening the refrigerator.

"Nope, just the same old broken promises," James deadpanned.

"Are you eating cereal? You sure the milk isn't spoiled?" Claudine asked sounding upset.

"It tastes fine to me. It's a little warm, but it's alright I guess."

"So why didn't you just finish it. You left a little sip in the carton when you should've just thrown it out," Claudine said getting angrier by the second. James looked at her before answering.

"I had enough milk in the bowl. I can't eat soggy cereal."

"James, are you fucking kidding me? There's not enough milk in here for a roach to get a gulp. I don't why you always do that. You know I hate it."

"Now hold up, did you want some milk?"

"Maybe, yes! But I saw a carton in there. If you had thrown it out, I would've automatically ruled out anything having to do with milk."

"Just a second ago, you were asking me if I'm sure whether or not the milk was spoiled, like you were concerned about my well-being. I'm sorry. Did you want some spoiled milk too? Or was that just your way of setting up a fight?"

"I'm not trying to start a fight with you, James. I'm just saying…"

"What're you saying? Look, I know you aggie and pissed off about everything but don't put that on me," James said getting up and walking to the window. He seemed to be getting wound up too, and didn't want to go through another day like yesterday. He thought for a minute before continuing.

"I'm tired of drinking lukewarm water as much as the next man. I know you'd like to nothing better but to go in your air-conditioned room, turn on your computer, and do your thing. But hey, the entire city of New York is with you."

"James, don't try to analyze me, please! You don't know what I want or what I need. You're the one in here by yourself drinking spoiled milk. Since when did you ever eat cereal in the middle of the afternoon?"

"Hey, at least I can admit that this shit is driving me crazy, but you? Oh no," James said letting caution go.

He tiptoed long enough. Claudine and James were now locked in a full-blown argument. She stomped out and James was behind her shouting at the top of his lungs. They continued loudly arguing and were walking back and forth in the apartment. Finally retuning to the kitchen, James picked up a cup and filled it water.

"I can't argue with you anymore, alright. So why don't you just cool off," James said.

He dumped the cup of water on her head before Claudine could get her response in. Claudine was stunned and remained speechless for a minute. Then she started laughing hysterically. James was now shocked at her reaction.

"Okay, now I know you done lost your mind. I swear, the heat has fried your brain," Claudine said.

Claudine went for a cup, filled it with water and returned the favor. They were both laughing and a water fight was on. After awhile, they were on good terms again. James kissed Claudine passionately and they settled down on the sofa hugging each other. They were exhausted from the water fight and both realized they truly loved each other.

"When all this drama clears, we're going to put an emergency kit together, complete with batteries, flashlights, travel pack, foods…"

"Okay, hold up GI Jane, how much are we talking here? Last

time this happened you were just barely born. You just love to debate, don't you?"

"Isn't that why you love me? Because I'm not some hood rat from around the way with no thought-provoking issues to stimulate your mind," Claudine said running her hand over James' back.

"No, on the contrary, I love you because you're a well-spoken hood rat who stimulates me in bed," James laughed.

"Well, we're not in bed now and it seems like you're stimulated to me," Claudine laughed and playfully punched James in the face.

They kissed again, and it was deeper and more passionate this time. He could feel the hunger for her growing deep in his stomach. She held him tightly. James was ready to love her. He didn't want to let her go. Claudine slipped out of his arms and ran to bedroom.

"I want you back in bed, Mr. Man," she laughed.

James jumped on the bed with Claudine and kissed her fervently. He held her so that she couldn't run. He looked intently in her eyes and grew serious as he realized how beautiful she was and how much he loved her. He swallowed hard, realizing how much they could have lost during the blackout.

"I'm gonna be real with you, baby. I don't know how much more of this I can take," James said looking her eyes.

A look of disappointment appeared on Claudine's face.

"You're telling me that you feel like I'm teasing you?" she

asked running her hand over his hair.

"No, baby, that's not what I'm talking about. I would just like things to be normal again. I am just sick of no electricity and stores being closed..."

"Oh, James, you can't back out on me now. You've been keeping me going this far. You've got to stay with me, c'mon now."

Their lips met again and she pulled him down on top of her. James felt her soft caramel skin quivering with the flickering of his tongue. Holding her frame tightly beneath his hard rock body, James entered her warm moisture, thrusting. She felt his manhood.

"James," Claudine softly cried and pulled him deep inside her.

So began an intense afternoon of lovemaking. She raked James' back with her manicured nails, hugging him real tight while biting his neck and kissing his lips. Claudine opened her legs wide in ecstasy, giving her entire body to her man. She gently rolled her hips and held him inside her. James massive thrusts were received by the soft cushioning of her belly. The smashing of their flesh was music that filled the entire apartment.

# TWENTY

4:30 p.m.

The barbershop crew returned to the block and lounged in front of the shop. It was hot and most of the residents were out on the street. Everyone was sweating profusely from the sweltering heat and lack of air conditioning. Even the police loosened their shirts and used their hats as fans. There was news that the power may be back on but so far it hadn't happened in the area.

"Yo Nel, let's go for a drive in your whip, man. And get out of the neighborhood," L suggested.

"Hell-to-the-muthafucking-no! Haven't you been listening, my brother?" Nelson asked staring at L. "The gas stations are all shut down. Let this shit go on for two or three more days and all these cats you see flossing down the strip is gonna be assed out. This here's some ol' *Mad Max Beyond Thunder Dome* in Brooklyn shit. I'm preserving my gas, you feel me?"

"It's not gonna get that crazy Nel," Cam said.

"Yeah? We'll see..." Nelson added.

WELCOME
TO
BROOKLYN

**5:00 p.m.**

In nearby Hallsboro Projects, the residents were frustrated not only by the blackout but also the lack of water. They also had to deal with the harassment of Wisdom and his goons who were holding down the entrance.

Two guys walking toward them stopped abruptly. Both looked around and were conscious that were about to cross paths with the gang. The two young men quickly made a beeline for a building before Wisdom or his goons spotted them.

After a few minutes, the gang became bored and prepared to leave.

"Wiz, where we going?" one of the goons asked.

"Da Bush, to rob the rich and bring back to the hood. Poor people can enjoy eatin'," Wisdom said without flinching.

WELCOME
TO
BROOKLYN

**5:10 p.m.**

Nel, Rick, Tech, L and Cam were taking in the side show caused by the blackout. With no traffic lights, the police were doing their best to direct traffic but confused motorists were still having problems. The booming of a car system blasted through the block and everyone was momentarily distracted by it. The bass was deafening and despite the temperature, heads were bobbing and people started to dance to the music. Kids on the streets were reciting the lyrics word for word. Even a young white cop on the corner couldn't resist joining in.

The sounds of Brooklyn royalty was coming through loud and clear. The voice of the Notorious B.I.G. was louder as the car got closer.

> *...I make it hot like a kettle get*
> *You delicate you better get who sent you*
> *You still peddle shit I got more rhymes than great*
> *adventure... Biggie...*
> *Kick in the door waving four-four...*
> *All you heard was Poppa don't hit me no more...*

**5:30 p.m.**

On the corner of Flatbush Avenue, a car made an abrupt stop at the intersection. The car's frame trembled from the bass pumping and the rap skills of B.I.G. on full blast for all to hear. There were four young men in the car. It was Wisdom and his goons from Hallsboro Projects.

The car made a right turn on Browser Street and stopped in front of the crew from the barbershop. Both groups shot cold stares at each other. Wisdom, while reciting the lyrics, threw up a gang sign and gave the barbershop crew the middle finger.

"Oh, come on. That dude a grown-ass man, trying to call me out like that," Nelson said.

"Fuck, I'm sayin' who he think he is? Boyz 'N the Hood?" Rick laughed.

"Word...that Biggie track is a hot classic, that's what's up. *Kick in the door/ waving the four-four all you heard was Poppa don't hit me no more...*" Cam sang along.

Finally the car peeled out and parked around the corner. The voice of the king of New York faded.

6:00 p.m.

The Hallsboro thugs walked to Ali's bodega on the corner of the block, looking for a vic. They were menacing and became the center of attention as they began disrespecting other people on the line.

Wisdom, to get immediate service, approached Ali. The people standing and waiting on line were becoming irritated with the goons' behavior. They were intimidated and did nothing but muttered under their breaths.

"Shut the fuck up, yo! I just want to see if the nigga selling water. Y'all lucky you even got water on this end. Go ahead with that!" Wisdom said to the people on line. "Boss man, you still selling water by the gallon?" he shouted at Ali.

"I got a few left but you can't skip the line, man. You got to get on line like everyone else," Ali said to Wisdom.

Wisdom paid no attention to what Ali was saying. He kept kept looking around in the store, scoping for a stickup.

"Nah, true that. I just wanted to check first before I got on line, that's all," Wisdom said.

**6:15 p.m.**

Tech and L were walking to the store when L saw a young black officer on the corner looking him up and down. It was the same cop from yesterday. Frustration combined with his exhaustion, and L reacted with fiery anger.

"Damn, man, why you grilling me like that? I ain't got no weed on me, what?" L asked, yelling at the officer.

"Excuse me?" the cop replied. He looked L up and down once

again then immediately pulled out his radio.

"You heard me, man! I'm just minding mines and you all in my grill like I'm some criminal," L said getting angrier. "Everyday y'all come in the hood hard body to beat down the Black man."

"Yo L, be easy. One hun'red, man be easy," Tech cautioned, pulling L back.

"No man, fuck that! I ain't having this bullshit. Plus I'm hungry," L said, trying to get out of Tech's grip.

"You want to make trouble for yourself?" the officer asked L, stepping closer to him.

The confrontation threatened to escalate and Tech acted quickly. In an attempt to defuse the situation, he pulled L in the other direction. L was livid and wasn't caving in to any kind of intervention, even from the police.

"Let me go, man. Let me tell this cat sump'n," L said trying to twist his way free of Tech's grasp.

"Officer, look we don't want no beef. It's been a long day and," Tech said to the officer while trying to hold an angry L in check.

"Why you gonna be looking me up, for? You think I'm just another nigga to throw in central booking, right? It's all the same. Yo man, let me tell you sump'n. This still a free country. This ain't no concentration camp. This Brooklyn!"

"C'mon man, you made your point, let's be out, L," Tech said pushing L back.

"I'm not bowing my head down when I walk these streets. Fuck you think this is?" L said fuming mad. Tech's hands were full trying to hold him back.

"If I was you, I'd bring my voice down," the officer said.

Other officers started to make their way over. The young cop saw the backup coming and he became more aggressive. L saw the other cops and decided to heed Tech's advice.

"If it wasn't for you, dog, I'd be going hard body fucking that cop up," L said walking away.

"And your ass be going to jail and probably catch a beat-down on the way, and that's one hun'red," Tech warned. "C'mon man, you be wilding out too much. If you want this music thing to work you best chill out. A lot of rappers in jail, you know."

6:20 p.m.

Nelson, Cam and Rick were on the line with the rest of the customers of Ali's grocery. Nelson had seen one of the goons from Hallsboro Projects parading in front of the store, and this drew his ire. Rick noticed the changed attitude.

"Nel, I'm sayin', man. What's wrong, man?" Rick asked.

"Look on the corner, that's that same Hallsboro cat right there that drove past that shop earlier, and my man is scheming hard. I ain't feeling that. Especially with what happened to CJ. Shit got me amped, you feel me?" Nelson said.

The goons looked over and saw Nelson eyeing them. Nelson was not backing down and when their stares locked, it was apparent that pretty soon sparks would start to fly.

"I know for a fact that niggas out here on this end. Don't know me like that to be all up in my face like I'm some ol' pretty lil' bitch!" one of the goons said.

Nelson did not make eye contact, but responded with anger to the comment anyway.

"Last time I checked, there were stores out in Hallsboro, so if Hallsboro niggas don't like getting grilled by Browser niggas, then y'all should stay the fuck off the block," Nelson said.

Other customers on line nodded in agreement. That didn't do anything to pacify situation. The combatants dug their heels and were ready for war.

"What, you trying to set shit off over here, nigga?" the goon asked with his chest puffed up.

6:30 p.m.

Cam and Rick left the line and followed behind Nelson.

Wisdom was about to make his move in the stick-up, but the altercation between them was about to derail the plan. Cam took off her T-shirt and wrapped it around her head, ready to get busy.

"Go ahead set it, pa," Nelson dared the goon.

Nelson and the goon stood toe to toe coldly staring each other down. Neither of them flinched as the restless crowd seemed to be dying for blood and pressed the war of words and into a physical confrontation. People were jumping atop cars to get a better view of the pending fight.

Wisdom pulled a gun from his waist and started to move on Nelson who was caught in a stare-down with another goon. L and Tech saw the growing crowd in front of the bodega. They recognized that Nelson was involved and started running toward their comrades. Wisdom closed in on Nelson, his face twisted with violent intentions. He held the gun cocked and ready to blast Nelson.

"Clap that fool, Wiz!" a goon shouted.

6:45 p.m.

Back in the bedroom of Claudine and James, they hugged and cuddled. Claudine was doing her best to console James.

"I have to say, going through this experience with you has

shown me that---"

Suddenly the television blared loudly from inside the living room. Claudine and James froze for minute staring at each other in disbelief.

"That's the TV!" he shouted.

"Oh my God, the power is back on!" Claudine screamed with incredulous joy.

There was a loud roar coming from the window. The people out in the streets and in their homes were shouting loudly, victoriously. It was as if the whole borough had awakened again. James and Claudine hugged and began dancing around.

6:47 p.m.

In front of the bodega, there was chaos. Before Wisdom was able to squeeze a shot off, the street lights flickered and motorists began blowing their horns. Air conditioners started whirling loudly. The Hallsboro menace put his gun away and the goons all scrambled out of the area as the celebration on Browser Street took over.

Residents came onto their fire escapes to chant and hoot as if they had won a championship game. Store vendors who had stayed out all day awaiting the return of power finally opened their stores.

"Thank God," a sweat-drenched police officer looked up and

sighed. After directing traffic all day, he was finally relieved.

7:00 p.m.

James and Claudine were still dancing around enjoying themselves. She was hugging him and kissing his face. Then she paused and pulled away quietly.

"Baby, is everything okay?" James asked as she started making motions to leave.

"I'm going outside for a few minutes, honey. I need to be out there," she answered smiling.

"You want me to go with you?" James asked with concern.

"No, baby, I'll be fine, really," she replied.

She walked back and gently touched his face. He pulled her close and they shared a deep, loving kiss. She whirled around and walked out of the apartment. James sighed watching her strange behavior, but gave up trying to figure her out.

# TWENTY ONE

7:05 p.m.

Out in the streets, music was blaring. People were still outside in front of the building but the tension had been swept away by the rush of electrical current. The sun was setting and a slight wind offered some relief from the humidity. Everything appeared to be cooling down and people returned slowly to their normal routine.

George and Sol walked out of the building. Sol's driver was parked out front waiting on him.

"Well, George, I guess this is it. Thank you for your hospitality," Sol said shaking George's hand.

"Oh, think nothing of it, Mr. Berman. It was my pleasure. I'm afraid it's been some time since I've had company, much less good company," George smiled, adjusting the cigar clinging to his lips.

"George, from now on just call me Sol, please."

"Okay, Sol," George laughed.

There was a pause before Sol spoke.

"Um, ah listen, George about the discussion we had last night,

I just wanted you to know...well, I've decided that I'm going to have the buildings renovated. You know? Keep things a bit more updated, so that the number of repairs needed could be reduced."

"Well that, ah... that's right. There's great news, Sol. I'm sure all of the tenants will be pleased to know," George said smiling.

"Yeah, I hope so. After all, I don't want them pestering my superintendent. You'll have your hands filled maintaining all of the renovations."

"That's right. Very true," George said, the smile on his face widening into laughter.

Sol and George shared a firm handshake. There was new found respect between the two men.

"You're a good man, George. A good man," Sol said patting George's shoulder.

"Thank you, Sol. Likewise," George said.

Sol made his way to the passenger side of the car. Before getting inside, Sol looked back at George.

"Please keep me personally updated with everything. If there's anything you need, if you have any problems, please do not hesitate to call me, okay?"

"Will do, will do. Thank you," George said waving.

Claudine walked out of the building and George turned to see her standing behind him.

"Hey, George," Claudine greeted.

"Hey there, pretty lady," George said greeting the pensive Claudine. "How're you feeling?"

"Better now, I guess. Is it me, or does it feel just a bit cooler now?" Claudine asked looking around.

George looked her up and down, and a subtle laugh of relief escaped his lips. He gently placed his hand on Claudine's shoulder then walked back into the building. Claudine smiled but felt like she missed something. James walked up behind and hugged her.

"Where are you going, James?" Claudine asked.

"To the store," James replied.

Together they stared at the spot where CJ was found dead and the shrine erected in his memory.

"What are you gonna get at the store, baby?" Claudine asked.

"I'm gonna get some milk," James said, smiling and walking away. Claudine shared the smile.

"Be back soon...I'm gonna visit CJ's mom." Caludine said going into the building.

Around 7:30 p.m. Reggie walked by them and went inside the building. He walked up the stairs and rapped on Fatima's door.

"I came to get my stuff," he said when she came to the door.

"Okay, you can get it," she said allowing the door to open.

Reggie walked in and all his stuff was neatly packed and placed in the center of the living room, ready to go. He chuckled and shook his head.

"You're really kicking me out, huh? For what...?" Reggie asked acting mystified.

"You're not for me, Reggie. You've proven it. Now just get out."

"But Fatima don't I get a chance to explain?"

"Explain what, Reggie? I have had a chance to think about it and I think this is for the best."

"It's you I love, but this girl won't leave me alone."

"Please, get out. You're sounding pathetic," Fatima said holding the door open.

"Where can I go?" Reggie asked while struggling to lift his suitcases out the apartment.

"I don't care where you go. I'm sure she won't let you stay in the hallway," Fatima said.

"I paid for half the TV," Reggie said.

"I really don't give a damn, Reggie," Fatima said and slammed the door.

Standing in the hallway, Reggie thought about his situation for a beat. Then he picked up his belongings and started up the stairs.

**7:45 p.m.**

Sol got in his car and sat in the passenger side. He wiped the sweat off his forehead.

"Boss, it's good to see you. Are you okay? How did you make out last night?" Tony asked.

"I'm fine. Everything worked out just fine," Sol replied.

"I'm really sorry about that you know. I mean leaving you out here. With the power gone, I had no way of reaching you. Then I thought it might be dangerous if I returned, or maybe you might have taken a cab or…"

"Anthony, don't worry about it. Everything's okay."

Anthony was relieved and a smile creased his lips. Sol watched him for a few beats.

"Okay…so how did things work out with George? Did you kick him out?" Anthony asked.

"Actually no…I had a change of heart. George will be staying. I learned a great deal about him over the course of the evening, and discovered that he is in fact an asset to me. However, I am contemplating firing you for leaving my ass stranded out here yesterday," Sol said with an evil smirk on his face.

Anthony gave Sol a nervous smile.

"Are we gonna sit here forever, or are you gonna get me the hell out of here today?" Sol asked.

"Yes, boss," the terrified chauffer said as the car screeched away.

7:50 p.m.

Claudine took a stroll through the neighborhood. Tech was outside the barbershop hustling CDs and bootleg DVDs. Claudine walked along the strip taking in all the sights. Things seemed back to normal, she thought as she saw Tech and his customers haggling over prices. She stopped and took in a deep breath, relieved that all the drama had ended. It had been a rough twenty-four hours for her.

There were more vendors out on the street trying to make up for the time lost. Customers were eager to spend money. Brooklyn was back to being the place it usually was.

7:55 p.m.

Ali opened the gate to the bodega, and customers rushed in to purchase items they so badly needed. Fatima walked in the store and Ali hurried to greet her.

"Hey, Fatima," Ali said with a friendly smile.

"Hey, Ali," Fatima responded.

"I guess your little surprise evening was ruined last night, huh?" Ali asked making conversation.

Fatima paused and looked away. She was trying to hide the hurt she felt even though she knew she couldn't.

"In more ways than you can imagine," she said after a few beats.

"I'm sure you can make it up another day," Ali said.

"I'm afraid yesterday's blackout actually shed light in one home last night. Reggie and I are no longer together."

Ali was taken aback. He did not know what to say and for a minute there was dead silence. She paid for the items.

"Really?" he asked too excitedly. He paused admiring her beautiful features and saw the sadness in her brown eyes. "I mean for real? I'm sorry to hear that."

"I'm not sorry," Fatima said coldly. "Take care, Ali."

"Um…ah, Fatima, listen, you know, from one poet to another, maybe some time you and I can catch some spoken word downtown. Have some dinner, you know? Get to know each other outside of this element."

"Wow, Ali, I'm flattered. Are you asking me out?" Fatima asked in surprise.

"Yeah, I mean, I was respecting your boy. But if he was stupid enough to do something to lose a gem like yourself, I can't just sit back and let you get lost or swept up in some deep sands...like the pestilence of..."

"Alright Ali, that's enough poetry. Wow, I mean I never looked at you that way, Ali," she said walking away.

"Alright then," Ali said waving and trying to hide his disappointment.

He was standing at the entrance when she walked back and smiled. He returned her smile. Then his big surprise came.

"Okay, Ali, okay. Here's my number. Give me a call," Fatima smiled and said.

Ali fumbled for something sensible to say, but was at a loss for words. He just kept smiling. He tried to suppress the excitement coursing through his entire being.

"I'll call. I'll do that," he said as Fatima walked out of the store and waved. "Bye."

"Thank you, Allah. Thank you..." Ali intoned, palms raised.

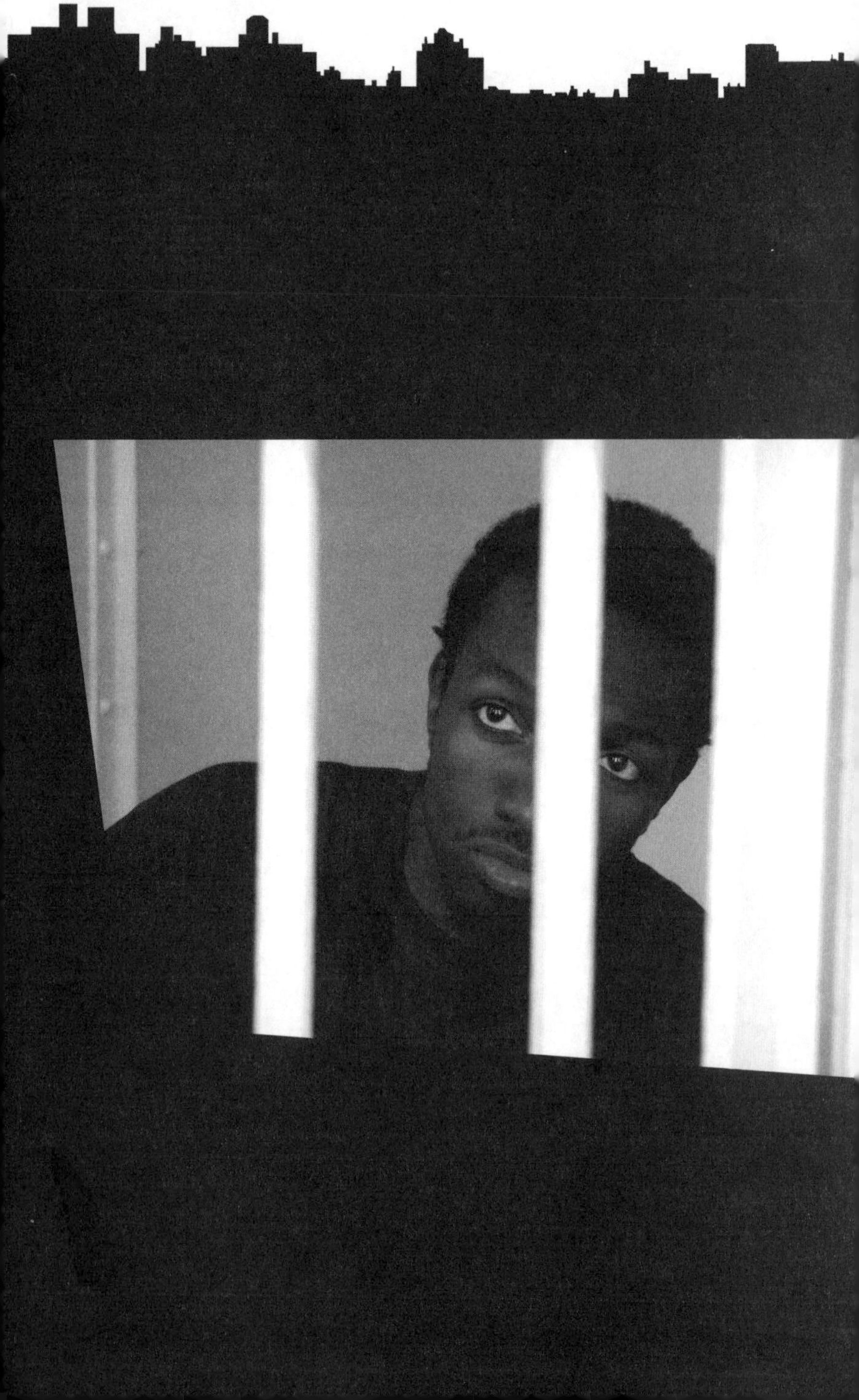

# TWENTY TWO

**Friday, August 15, 8:15 p.m.**

The streets of East Flatbush were flooded with people. Children played under the spray of hydrants while others ran around. The barbershop was back to business as usual. Customers tried to get a fresh haircut for the weekend, while others stood outside enjoying the evening. All the fellas stared at Shay-Shay as she went by. Tech was still hustling his wares. The West Indian women were out front at 254 Browser Street with their lawn chairs, gossiping. It was as if Thursday night didn't happen.

Claudine walked back to the building and stopped alongside a group that stood intently watching the news broadcast given by Mayor Bloomberg and Police Commissioner Ray Kelly at City Hall.

*"People of New York City, once again we've prevailed. We've shown that we can overcome adversity. Power has officially been restored in the city. With the exception of a few minor, sporadic incidents, reports indicate that there have been very few cases of*

*looting, some fires, mostly as result of burning candles. There've been few, if any, violent accidents. New Yorkers were helpful, supportive and on their best behavior, proving that the power of the people of this city cannot and will not be broken…*

A chorus rained from the crowd. "Boo…! Boo…!"

Everyone standing around raised their arms and simultaneously shouted curses at the politician's attempt to downplay the tumultuous events of the past thirty hours. Claudine shook her head and walked up to the front of the building.

"Yo, they didn't even mention CJ," someone in the crowd shouted.

Claudine continued to soak it all in but was relieved that whole episode was over. She took a deep breath, made the sign of the cross while whispering a silent prayer, and walked past the shrine for CJ. Candles, flowers, cards and a picture of him decorated the tribute. Zoning out the loud gossiping women, Claudine sat down on the stoop in the front of the building and watched the kids play.

It was around 8:30 p.m. when Toothless Tone walked slowly by the building pushing his cart. Claudine noticed him as he stopped at the shrine. Aside from Claudine, he was one of the few faces in the crowd not smiling. Toothless Tone fell to his knee as if in prayer.

"Look at them," he muttered looking around at the people. "Just look at them all, smiling and laughing. My, my, my, how quickly we forget. Nobody listens, nobody cares. They just laugh like helpless fools. Nobody wants to look further than what's in front of them. Ignorance is bliss. To them, it's just another day in the ghetto…"

Toothless Tone lifted his head to sky. With his arms outstretched, he shouted at the top of his lungs.

"For God so love the world that He gave His only begotten son for whosoever believeth in him shall have everlasting life…"

9:15 p.m.

Inside a lock-up at a Brooklyn north precinct, several young men were being processed through the system. They were getting fingerprinted and having mug shots taken. Khalil, his face filled with remorse, stared silently into dire prospects. Officers were marching in prisoner after prisoner.

Khalil was roughly ushered into the cell with all the others. He seemed to be taking it in stride but had never thought this far ahead of the game and wasn't ready for it. He sat thinking about all the opportunities that would pass him and his friends by. All the terrible things he shouldn't have done came to the forefront of his mind. Ty had quit school to be a thug like Rasheed. Now he was dead and Khalil was locked in a bullpen. They all should've listened to CJ.

Maybe it wasn't too late.

**9:30 p.m.**

Inside the emergency waiting area of Kings County Hospital, Rasheed was cuffed to a gurney inside of a crowded city hospital. His face contorted in pain. Wounded but not a priority, he was no longer the center of attention. Doctors walked by him as he winced and cried out in pain. Cell bars would be his only reward. His relief would not arrive for hours yet. Rasheed closed his eyes.

**10:00 p.m.**

"Devon, come on in now," a mother shouted.

Kids playing in front of 254 Browser Street scuttled off to their respective homes. Inside her first floor apartment, Ms. Thompson sat in her bedroom quietly listening to the clamoring coming from the street. She was exhausted but couldn't rest. Her mind wouldn't let her. Dark clouds seemed to have swooped down and stolen CJ. Now she wanted to get up and run, scream, shake her fist at the world, but she stayed inside lamenting.

The modest two-bedroom apartment appeared emptier and lonelier, now that CJ was no longer there. The blackout had wiped him off the earth. He continued living in her heart, but still she missed his smile. Ms. Thompson pulled out a pile of pictures of CJ that traced his life from toddler to his most recent high school graduation. She had worked hard to raise him, now it seemed like it was all for naught. She knelt at the side of her bed and prayed for her son's killers.

Ms. Thompson's thoughts were interrupted by the sounds of the street. Toothless Tone's angry rants wafted up through her window. She could hear young babies crying and the loud laughter of playing children. Ms. Thompson heard a knock at her door. All day long she avoided attempts to reach her. The knocking continued and Ms. Thompson tried but could no longer ignore it. She took a deep breath and slowy walked to the door. Biting her lips, she reluctantly opened it. .

"George," she sighed in relief. "Please, come on in."

"Hi Layla," he said plucking the cigar from his lips and producing a bouquet of yellow roses. "I'm so sorry about CJ..." he started and hugged her so tightly, his lips went dry. George cleared his throat holding back the tears. Ms Thompson's body heaved with emotion against him and she sobbed silently.

WELCOME
TO
**BROOKLYN**

**10:15 p.m.**

Street lights and air-conditioners buzzed. Claudine sat outside on the stoop in front of the building. With a blank stare, she watched young girls placing flowers and cards on CJ's shrine. Claudine had tried visiting Ms. Thompson but there was no answer. She evidently wanted to be alone. Claudine sighed her understanding and shook her head as her thoughts returned to the tragic affair.

She hadn't been prepared for all the craziness that occurred as a result of the blackout. Claudine was stressed trying to make sense of the chaos in her community, she remained profoundly disturbed. She had witnessed firsthand people in Manhattan helping others, and she expected the same in her neighborhood. It wasn't. This was a disheartening slice of life she had to digest. CJ's death was devastating. The revival of her relationship with James was the only good outcome of the mess.

A little way off from the steps of the building, Claudine watched an exhausted Toothless Tone sitting on the sidewalk. He pulled out a muffin and began eating. Smiling, he glanced around, shaking his head and shouting.

"Long as the sun keeps shining life will keep moving, cuz this Brooklyn..."

# EPILOGUE

Claudine Rivera sat her desk in the office of Uptown Magazine carefully tracing her thoughts into an article about the last 48 hours. She was trying to recreate her experience without leaving her personal feelings.

"Make it as straightforward as possible without any of your prejudices," the editor had asked.

"I'll do my best," Claudine answered.

She was filled with excitement walking back to her computer and thinking of the possible angle of the piece. Claudine felt the adrenaline rushing through her nervous fingers tapping the keyboard.

*Thursday, August 14, 2003.*

*No one could imagine that a sequence of electrical mishaps would trigger the worst blackout in the U.S. history. Millions of Americans in the northeast were without power for up to forty-eight hours. In New York City, the first window broke on Flatbush Avenue in Brooklyn, at about 4:20 p.m. on August 14, 2003, about 10 minutes after the blackout began.*

*Some New Yorkers were in shock and compared the catastrophic event to 9/11. Many were prepared and worked to help fellow New Yorkers. While others were not in such a giving mood, looters were out, price gouging was rampant and accidental fires were severe...*

# BlacKout

Lights Out
Woken by fire
The smell of defeat
Visions of hopes and dreams
Float away in smoke
And every word
Is like an unnecessary stain
On silence and nothingness
Discreetly mounted
On the faces of victims
Identities misplaced
Surrounded by darkness
A black box
In a bright world
It's a BLACKOUT

poem by
Lesley Blair Winchester

# BlacKout

Cast and Crew

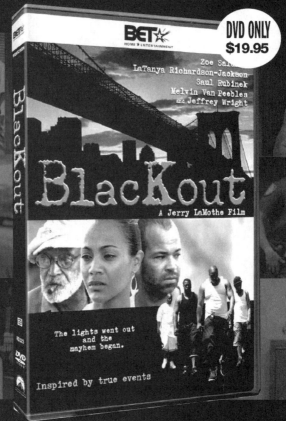

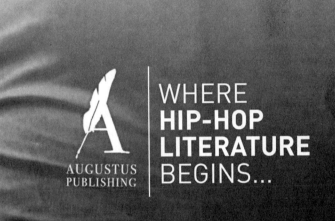

# WHERE
# HIP-HOP
# LITERATURE
BEGINS...

**AUGUSTUS PUBLISHING**

Augustus Publishing was created to unify minds with entertaining, hard-hitting tales from a hood near you. Hip Hop literature interprets contemporary times and connects to readers through shared language, culture and artistic expression. From street tales and erotica to coming-of age sagas, our stories are endearing, filled with drama, imagination and laced with a Hip Hop steez

# GHETTO GIRLS I

*Young Luv*

**Ghetto Girls IV Young Luv**
$14.95 // 9780979281662

**Ghetto Girls**
$14.95 // 0975945319

**Ghetto Girls Too**
$14.95 // 0975945300

**Ghetto Girls 3 Soo**
$14.95 // 0975945351

THE BEST OF THE STREET CHRONICLES TODAY, THE **GHETTO GIRLS SERIES** IS A WONDERFULLY HYPNOTIC ADVENTURE THAT DELVES INTO THE CONVOLUTED MINDS OF CRIMINALS AND THE DARK WORLD OF POLICE CORRUPTION. YET, THERE IS SOMETHING THRILLING AND SURPRISINGLY TENDER ABOUT THIS ONGOING YOUNG-ADULT SAGA FILLED WITH MAD FLAVA.

## Love and a Gangsta
author // **ERICK S GRAY**

This explosive sequel to **Crave All Lose All**. Soul and America were together ten years 'til Soul's incarceration for drugs. Faithfully, she waited four years for his return. Once home they find life ain't so easy anymore. America believes in holding her man down and expects Soul to be as committed. His lust for fast money rears its ugly head at the same time America's musi career takes off. From shootouts, to hustling and thugging life, Soul and his man, Omega, have done it. Omega is on the come-up in the drug-game of South Jamaica, Queens. Using ties to a Mexican drug cartel, Omega has Queens in his grip. His older brother, Rahmel, was Soul's cellmate in an upstate prison Rahmel, a man of God, tries to counsel Soul. Omega introduces New York to crystal meth. Misery loves company and on the road to the riches and spoils of the game, Omega wants the only man he can trust, Soul, with him. Love between Soul and America is tested by an unforgivable greed that leads quickly to deception and murder.

**$14.95** // 9780979281648

 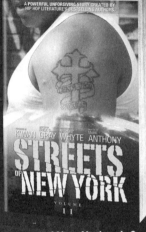 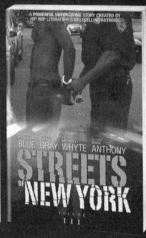

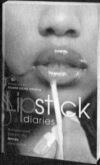